Daniel C. Eddy

Christian Heroines

Lives and Sufferings of Female Missionaries in Heathen Lands

Daniel C. Eddy

Christian Heroines
Lives and Sufferings of Female Missionaries in Heathen Lands

ISBN/EAN: 9783337193690

Printed in Europe, USA, Canada, Australia, Japan

Cover: Foto ©Lupo / pixelio.de

More available books at **www.hansebooks.com**

New Editions of Popular Books.

IN SETS.

THE YOUNG LADIES' LIBRARY,

CONSISTING OF

PAPERS FOR THOUGHTFUL GIRLS. By Sarah M. Tytler.
THE YOUNG WOMAN'S FRIEND. By Daniel C. Eddy, D. D.
CHRISTIAN HEROINES. By Daniel C. Eddy, D. D.

This series of books is presented to the trade in a new dress, and the volumes confidently offered as being among the most popular thoughtful and religious books for girls and young ladies ever published. More than one hundred and thirty thousand volumes of the series have been sold. 3 vols., 16mo., Cloth, black and gold, in a box, . . $4.50

THE CARLETON SERIES,

CONSISTING OF

WINNING HIS WAY,   FOLLOWING THE FLAG,
MY DAYS AND NIGHTS ON THE BATTLE FIELD.

By Charles Carleton Coffin, author of "The Boys of '76," "The Story of Liberty," "Our New Way 'Round the World," etc.

These remarkably interesting books having been long out of print, and there being a large demand for them, we shall issue new and uniform editions in an attractive form. 3 vols., 16mo., Cloth, in a neat box, ... $3.75

THE LEGAL ADVENTURE LIBRARY,

CONSISTING OF

THE EXPERIENCES OF A BARRISTER. By Samuel Warren, author of "Ten Thousand a Year."
RECOLLECTIONS OF A POLICEMAN. By Thomas Waters, of the London Detective Corps.
THE ADVENTURES OF AN ATTORNEY IN SEARCH OF PRACTICE. By Sir James Stephen.

3 vols., 12mo., Cloth, in a neat box, ... $3.75

THE NEW ADVENTURE LIBRARY,

CONSISTING OF

ROCKY MOUNTAIN LIFE, PERILOUS ADVENTURES IN THE FAR WEST. By Rufus B. Sage.
JACK IN THE FORECASTLE. Incidents in the life of Hawser Martingale.
ROVINGS ON LAND AND SEA. By Captain Henry E. Davenport.

3 vols., 12mo., Cloth, in a neat box, ... $3.75

Sent postpaid on receipt of price by the publishers, ESTES & LAURIAT,
Boston, Mass.

CHRISTIAN HEROINES;

OR,

LIVES

AND

Sufferings of

Female Missionaries

In Heathen Lands.

BY DANIEL C. EDDY, D.D.

"There are deeds which should not pass away,
And names that must not wither."

NEW EDITION.

BOSTON:
ESTES AND LAURIAT,
301 TO 305 WASHINGTON STREET.
1881.

Entered, according to Act of Congress, in the year 1856, by

HORACE WENTWORTH,

In the Clerk's Office of the District Court of the District of Massachusetts

CONTENTS.

CHAPTER I.

HARRIET NEWELL.

PAGE

The crusade. Martin II. Peter the hermit. Missionary enterprise. Andover. The young men. Congregational association. American Board. Harriet Atwood. Bradford Academy. Conversion. Church in Haverhill. Death of her father. Samuel Newell. Marriage. Sailing. The Caravan. Salem harbor. Calcutta. Birth of the babe. Its death. Mrs. Newell dies. . 11

CHAPTER II.

ANN H. JUDSON.

Bradford. Ann Hasseltine. Harriet Atwood. Conversion. Communion. Marries Mr. Judson. Sails for Calcutta. Serampore. Change of views. Baptism. First child. First conversion. Trials and suffering. Judson's imprisonment. English government. Mrs. Judson dies. Amherst. The hopia tree. . 43

CHAPTER III.

ELIZABETH HERVEY.

Park Street Church. Ordination. Charge. The Corvo. Church in Hadley. Sermon. Labor. Death. 73

CHAPTER IV.

HARRIET B. STEWART.

Sandwich Islands. Opukakia. Sabbath scene. Stamford, Connecticut. Marriage. Lahaina. Death of Mrs. Stewart. Church-building at Waiakea. 97

CHAPTER V.

SARAH L. SMITH.

Syria. Norwich, Connecticut. John Robinson. New heart. Mohegan Indians. Brig George. Malta. Beyroot. The Mediterranean. Jerusalem. Sickness. Death. Burial service. . . 117

CHAPTER VI.

ELEANOR MACOMBER.

Lake Pleasant. Ojibwas. Dong-Yahn. Mr. Osgood. Zuagaben Mountains. Karens. Rev. Mr. Stephens. Church planted. The close. 133

CHAPTER VII.

SARAH D. COMSTOCK.

The Burman empire. Brookline. Baldwin Place Church. Mr. Wade. Dr. Wayland's address. Mrs. Sigourney. The Cashmere. Kyouk Phyoo. Mr. Kincaid. Six men for Arracan. "O Jesus, I do this for thee." Last illness. Lowly sepulchres. 163

CHAPTER VIII.

HENRIETTA SHUCK.

China. Rev. Addison Hall. Kilmarnock. Virginia revivals. Baptism. Death of her mother. Marriage to Mr. Shuck. Sea voyage. Ah Loo. Henrietta Layton. Premonitions. The end of earth. 183

CHAPTER IX.

SARAH B. JUDSON.

Alstead. Dr. Bolles. George D. Boardman. Poem. Discovery and subsequent union. Calcutta. Sarah Ann. Robbery. George. Death of Sarah. Ko Thah-byu. Rebellion. Boardman's death. Marriage to Mr. Judson. Poems. Death. Ex-Governor Briggs's speech. 203

CHAPTER X.

ANNIE P. JAMES.

Salem. Sarah Hall. Conversion. Consecration by public ordinance. Boardman Missionary Society. Meets Dr. James. Betrothal. Service in the First Church. Dr. Jewell's letter. Embarkation and voyage. Letters. Drowned. Testimonials. 239

CHAPTER XI.

EMILY C. JUDSON.

Early life. Alderbrook. Seminary at Utica. Writes for the New Mirror. The opinion of friends. Becomes acquainted with Dr. Judson. Prepares a memoir of Sarah B. Judson. Marriage. Sails to the East. Services on shipboard. Grief of friends. Labors in Burmah. Sickness of Dr. Judson. My bird. Dr. Judson sails on board the Aristide Marie. Dies at sea. Mrs. Judson returns to America. Superintends the memoirs of her late husband. Attends to his children, and dies. . . . 271

HEROINES OF THE CHURCH.

CHAPTER I.

HARRIET NEWELL,

THE PROTO-MARTYR.

SEVERAL centuries ago, the idea of driving out of Jerusalem its infidel inhabitants was suggested to a mad ecclesiastic. A shorn and dehumanized monk of Picardy, who had performed many a journey to that fallen city, who had been mocked and derided there as a follower of the Nazarene, whose heart burned beneath the wrongs and indignities which had been so freely heaped upon the head of himself and his countrymen, determined to arouse a storm which should send its lightnings to gleam along the streets, and roll its deep thunder to shake the hills which in speechless majesty stand around the city of God.

Pope Martin II. entered into his daring scheme, convened a council of bishops and priests, and gave the sanction of the church to the wild enterprise. This council Peter addressed, and, with all the eloquence of a man inspired by a mighty project, depicted the wrongs and grievances of those who yearly sought, for holy purposes, the sepulchre wherein the Savior of man reposed after his crucifixion. He was successful in inspiring the people with his own wild enthusiasm. All Europe flew to arms; all ranks and conditions in life united in the pious work; youthful vigor and hoary weakness stood side by side; the cross was worn upon the shoulder and carried on banners; the watchword, " *Deus Vult*," burst from ten thousand lips; and the armies of Christendom precipitated themselves upon the holy land with the awful war cry, " God wills it," echoing from rank to rank.

In later times a mightier, nobler enterprise was originated, and the great system of American missions commenced. The object was a grand one, and awfully important. It contemplated, not the subjection of a narrow kingdom alone, but the complete overthrow of the dark empire of sin; not the elevation of a human king, an earthly monarch, but the enthronement of an insulted God, as the supreme object of human worship; not the possession of the damp, cold sepulchre in which Jesus reposed after his melancholy death, but the erection of his cross on every hillside, by every sea shore, in vale and glen, in city and in solitude. It was a noble design, one full of grandeur and glory, as far surpassing the crusade of Peter the Hermit as the noonday sun surpasses the dim star of evening Its purpose was to obliterate the awful record of human sin, flash the rays of a divine illumination across a world of darkness, and send the electric thrill of a holy life throughout a universe of death.

At first, the missionary enterprise was looked upon as foolish and Utopian. Good men regarded it as utterly impracticable, and bad men condemned and denounced it as selfish and mercenary. The Christian church had not listened to the wail of a dying world as it echoed over land and ocean and sounded along our shores; she had not realized the great fact that every darkened tribe constitutes a part of the universal brotherhood of man; her heart had not been touched by the spirit of the great commission, " Go ye into all the world, and preach the gospel to every creature."

But the sun which ushered in the present century dawned upon a missionary age and a missionary church. The tide of time has floated man down to a region of light, and the high and holy obligations which rest upon the ransomed of God are being recognized. The question is now asked, with deep and serious earnestness,—

> " Shall we, whose souls are lighted
> By wisdom from on high,.
> Shall we to man benighted
> The lamp of life deny ? "

And the answer has been given. The church has felt, realized, and entered into her obligation. By the cross she has stood, her heart beating with kindly sympathy, her cheeks bathed in tears, and her lips vocal with prayer. The Macedonian cry has been heard, and from every nave, and alcove, and aisle, and altar of the great temple of Christianity has come the response, —

> "Waft, waft, ye winds, the story,
> And you, ye waters, roll,
> Till, like a sea of glory,
> Light spreads from pole to pole."

In the early part of the year 1808 several young men, members of the Divinity School at Andover, became impressed with the importance of a mission to the heathen world. They first looked on the subject at a distance, saw its dim and shadowy outlines, prayed that their visions of a converted world might be realized, and wondered who would go forth the first heralds of salvation. Ere long the impression came that *they* were the men; and in two years the impression had deepened into a solemn conviction, and they had determined on a life of labor, tears, and sacrifice.

In 1810 they made known their plans to an association of Congregational ministers assembled in Bradford. Although that body of holy men had many fears and some doubts concerning the success of the enterprise, no attempt was made to dampen the ardor of the young brethren who were resolved to undertake the vast work. Many of the aged men composing that association thought they could discern in the fervor and zeal of these young apostles of missions the inspiration of the Holy Ghost. However many were their fears and doubts, they dared not, as they loved the cross, place a single obstacle in the way of the accomplishment of such a lofty purpose, and when the question was asked by the sceptic, " Who is sufficient for these things ? " the awful response, " The sufficiency is of God," came up from many hearts.

This movement on the part of Messrs. Judson, Newell, Nott, and their associates, originated the American Board of Commissioners for Foreign Missions — an organization which has its mission stations in almost every part of the world, and which is expending, annually, the sum of two hundred thousand dollars for the conversion of the heathen. The first missionaries sent out were those above named, who, with two others, were ordained to the work in the Tabernacle Church, in Salem, on the 6th of February, 1812. The ordination scene is said to have been one of peculiar solemnity. The spectacle was an unusual one, and a vast crowd collected together. The spacious church, though filled to overflowing with excited and interested people, was as silent as the chamber of death as instructions were given to the young men who were to bid adieu to home and country. On the 19th of February, a cold, severe day, the brig Caravan moved down the harbor of Salem on an outward-bound voyage, bearing on her decks Messrs. Judson and Newell, with their wives, the others having sailed from Philadelphia for Calcutta the day previous. They went, not as the conqueror goes, with fire and sword, flowing banners and waving plumes, but as the heralds of salvation, having the gospel of life and peace to proclaim in the ears of men who were strangers to its glory. To portray the character of one of these devoted female missionaries, the wife of Samuel Newell, this sketch will be devoted.

Harriet Atwood was born in the town of Haverhill, on the sloping banks of the winding Merrimack, on the 10th of October, 1793. She was the daughter of Moses Atwood, a merchant of that village, who was universally respected and beloved. Though not rich, he was generous and benevolent; he was pious without affectation, and in his heart cherished a longing desire to do good. Her mother, who yet lives, was a woman of strong religious principle, and well calculated to give right direction to the opening mind of her child. Her piety, it is said, was of that kind which makes its impression upon the heart and conscience, and leads the beholder to admire and love. She was a fit mother to train such a daughter for her holy mission to a world in ruins, and, by her judicious advice and counsel, lead on her child to that high point of mental and moral advancement from whence she could look abroad upon a fallen race and pity human woe.

Throughout life Harriet Newell bore the marks, and carried the impressions, of childhood and youth, and her short but brilliant career was moulded and fashioned by her missionary-hearted mother.

In 1805 she entered upon a course of study at the Bradford Academy, and soon distinguished herself as a quick and ready scholar. One of her fellow-pupils remarks that "she seldom entered the recitation room unprepared. She seemed to take peculiar pains in doing things *well;* and though much of her time was spent in reading, her standing in her class was always more than respectable." Though but a child at this time, she kept a diary which would have done no discredit to a person of mature years, in which she recorded the exercises of her own mind and the progress which she made in mental discipline. The entries made in that diary give us an idea of the superiority of her mind and the excellency of her heart.

While at Bradford, her heart was renewed by the grace of God. During a revival which performed its holy work among the members of the school, she was led to view herself as a sinner against the

Almighty. The awful fact that she must be born again uttered its solemn admonition. Though not so deeply convicted as are some persons, she felt the terrible necessity of regeneration. Reason, conscience, and Scripture proclaimed the same truth; and after struggling against her better feelings for a while, she yielded herself in sweet submission to the will of God. The account which she gives of her own exercises of mind, while in this condition, furnishes us with a view of her real character. Her religious experience was full of feelings and acts characteristic of herself; and we may form our opinion of her disposition and cast of mind from the peculiarity of her religious emotions. In extreme youth she was fond of gayety and mirth, and spent much time in dancing. According to her own account, she had but little remorse of conscience for her thoughtless course. The fact that such amusements were sinful, as well as dangerous, had never been impressed upon her mind. She deemed them consistent with the highest state of moral and religious enjoyment, and pursued the miserable phantom of human, earthly pleasure, until aroused by the Spirit and made sensible of sin.

From early youth she had been accustomed to revere and study the word of God and pray to her Father in heaven for the things which she needed. Her pious parents had impressed the lessons of virtue on her young heart, and she was accustomed, as she arose in the morning and rested her head at night, to commend the keeping of her body and soul to the care of an overruling, superintending Providence; but after commencing the practice of dancing, and beginning to attend schools where this vain practice was learned, she neglected the Bible, and thought but little of the place of prayer. She found, after retiring at evening from the gay and fascinating scenes of the dancing room, that prayer and meditation were dull and tedious exercises, and concluded to give them up. Closing the Bible, she laid it aside, and let it gather dust upon the shelf, while vain and trifling volumes engaged her attention. The door of her closet was closed, and she entered it not; and all thoughts of God were banished from her mind, while the world employed all her time. But God, who orders all things, was about to perform on her heart a work of mercy and grace. She was a chosen vessel to bear the name of Jesus to a land of darkness and despair.

When about thirteen years of age, she was sent by her parents to the Academy at Bradford, to receive a systematic course of instruction. Shortly after this a revival of religion commenced, and spread through the school, and many were converted. The attention of Miss Atwood was arrested and turned from vanity. "Must I be born again?" was the searching question which she put to her own heart. The answer came to her, and she began to seek the Savior. She seems not to have had deep conviction; her mind, though agitated, was not overwhelmed, and the subject was contemplated calmly. At length, with the melancholy fact that she was a sinner, and endless condemnation before her, she was pointed to the cross of Christ. The view was effectual. Jesus appeared the Savior of sinners, of whom she was one, and faith gladly laid hold on him as the way of escape from an awful death. A wonderful change took place: she lost her love of folly and sin; prayer was sweet again; the Bible was drawn from its resting-place and perused with new pleasure; from both Bible and closet she derived pleasure such as she had never before experienced; and she passed from a state of nature to a state of grace.

Writing to her friends while in this mood of mind, she is willing to admit that she has not had such an overwhelming view of the nature of sin as some have, nor of the ecstatic joy which some experience on conversion; but she had what was as good — a calm hope in the merits of a crucified Savior, a high estimate of religion and religious privileges, and an utter contempt for the pleasures and vanities of the world. She had a holy love for all things good, and was able to

"Read or title clear
To mansions in the sky."

At the time when Miss Atwood found this sweet and precious hope, the church in Haverhill was in a low and languishing condition, disturbed by internal divisions, and to a great extent destitute of the influences of the Holy Spirit. In consequence of this state of the church she did not unite herself with it, and at that time made no open profession of religion. This neglect of a plain and obvious duty brought darkness upon her mind, and shrouded her soul in gloom. God withdrew his presence from his wayward and disobedient child, and left her in sadness: she had refused to confess her Master openly and publicly in the midst of trials and discouragements; and, grieved and wounded by her conduct, he turned from her, and hid his face. Then was she in the condition of the man who took into his own house seven spirits more wicked than himself. There was no rest for her soul, no relief for her anguished spirit. She realized how bitter a thing it is to depart from the counsel of her Maker, and found momentary comfort only in the forgetfulness of what she had enjoyed. At this period conscience was awake, and to drown its voice she plunged into sin, sought pleasure in all the departments of worldly intercourse, and thought as little as possible of God and sacred things. In this attempt to drive away serious inquiries she succeeded, and became as thoughtless as before her conversion. Again was the Bible laid aside, and the sickly novel and the wild romance substituted in its place. The closet was neglected, and she loved not to retire and commune with God. The flame of piety in her soul went out, and her heart was dark and sad; she fearfully realized the truth of the divine declaration, " The way of the transgressor is hard." In her diary she tells of sleepless nights and anxious days; of the Savior wounded by her whom he died to save; of the Spirit grieved, and almost quenched, yet lingering around her, now reproving, now commanding, now pleading; at one time holding up the terrors of a broken law, and then whispering in tones as sweet and gentle as Calvary; of conscience holding up a mirror in which she might discern the likeness of herself and contemplate her real moral character. Thoughts of God and holiness, of Christ and Calvary, made her gloomy and unhappy; and she entered the winding path of sin, that the celestial light might not burst upon her. Like other sinners, she sought happiness by forgetting what she was doing and by an entire withdrawal from all scenes which could awaken in her soul emotions of contrition and repentance.

On the 28th of June, 1809, Miss Atwood listened to a discourse, which was the instrument, in the hands of God, of again prostrating her at the foot of the cross. Her carnal security gave way; her sins, her broken vows and pledges, rose up before her in startling numbers; her guilt hung over her like a dark mantle; she felt the awful pangs of remorse, and was induced to return to that kind and compassionate Savior who had at first forgiven all her faults. Peace was restored; the smile of God returned; and the bleeding heart, torn and wounded by sin, had rest.

While in her fifteenth year, the subject of this sketch was called upon to part with her father. What influence this sad event had upon her mind is hardly known; but that it was an occasion of deep and thrilling anguish cannot be doubted. Smarting under the hand of Providence, she writes letters to several of her friends, which abound in words of holy and pious resignation. The manner in which her sire departed, his calm exit from the sorrows of the flesh, served to give her a more lofty idea of the power of faith to sustain its subject in the hour of death. Though he had left nine fatherless children and a broken-hearted widow, there was to Harriet a melancholy pleasure in the idea that he had burst off the fetters of clay and ascended to the skies. Though on earth deprived of his companionship, his counsels, and his guidance, she looked forward to a meeting where parting scenes will not be found, and where the farewell word will never be spoken.

"There is a world above,
 Where parting is unknown,
A long eternity of love,
 Formed for the good alone;

> And faith beholds the dying here
> Translated to that glorious sphere."

Nor had she a single doubt that her father had reached that world. She knew the sincerity, piety, and devotion of his life, and the sweet calmness of his death. His coffin, his shroud, his grave, his pale form were reposing in lonely silence beneath the bosom of the earth; but the spirit had departed on its journey of ages, and she doubted not its perfect felicity. As often as she repaired to the spot where he was interred, and kneeled by his tomb and breathed forth her humble supplications, she found the sweet assurance that beyond the grave she would see her earthly parent, and live with him forever. Though divided by the realms of space, faith carried her onward to the scenes of eternity and upward to the joys of heaven; and though she roamed on earth, shedding many a tear of sorrow, her spirit held communion with the spirit of her departed sire.

> "While her silent steps were straying
> Lonely through night's deepening shade,
> Glory's brightest beams were playing
> Round the happy Christian's head."

In October, 1810, an event occurred which gave direction to the whole life of Harriet Atwood. She became acquainted with Samuel Newell, one of the enthusiastic apostles of missions. He made her familiar with his plans and purposes, and asked her to accompany him as his colaborer and companion. Long had she prayed that she might be a source of good to her fellow-creatures; long had she labored to accomplish something for God and his holy cause; but the idea of leaving mother and friends, home and kindred, and going forth to preach salvation and tell of Jesus in wild and barbarous climes, was new and strange. To the whole matter she gave a careful and prayerful consideration. She divested the great subject as far as possible from all romantic drapery, and looked upon it in its true light. For a while her mind was in a state of perplexing doubt and fear, and the thought of leaving her own land was terrible. While considering the conflict in her mind, we should remember that the cause of missions was in its infancy; that no one had ever gone forth from our shores to preach salvation by grace in heathen countries; that those who were agitating the subject were branded as fanatics, and the cause itself was subject to unjust suspicions and contempt; consequently the subject had an importance and awfulness which it does not now possess. The way has been broken, and all good men acknowledge that the heroism of the missionary woman is grand and sublime. The decision made by Harriet Atwood was different from that made by others in after years, inasmuch as she had no example, no pattern. She realized that the advice of friends, biased as it was by prejudice and affection, could not be relied upon; and, driven to the throne of God, she wrestled there until her course of action was decided and her mind fixed intently upon the great work before her. Her resolution to go to India was assailed on every side. Those to whom she had been accustomed to look for advice and counsel, friends on whose judgment she had relied, shook their heads and gave decided tokens of disapprobation. But the question was finally settled. On one side were the gay world, her young associates, her kind relatives, her own care and comfort. On the other side stood a bleeding Savior and a dying world. To the question, "Lord, what wilt thou have me to do?" she heard the response, "Go work to day in my vineyard;" and when she looked forth upon the harvest, white for the reaper's hand, she hesitated not to consecrate on the altar of her God her services, her time, her life.

When this decision was once made, she conferred not with flesh and blood. Her reply was given to Mr. Newell in firm, decided language; and up to the hour when her spirit took its flight from earth to heaven, we have no evidence that she had one single regret that she had chosen a life of self-sacrifice. Her language was, —

> "Through floods and flames, if Jesus lead,
> I'll follow where he goes."

Through duties and trials, through floods and

flames, she passed, shrinking from no danger and shunning no sacrifice. Conscious of right, she quailed not before the tears of friends and the scorn of foes; but alike in duty and in danger followed the footsteps of her Savior, until her wasting body was decomposed and her spirit taken up to dwell with the just men made perfect.

To a friend in Beverly she writes as follows: "How can I go and leave those who have done so much for me, and who will be so sorry for my loss? How can I leave my mother here while oceans roll between us? How can I go with but little prospect of return? And how can I stay? We are under solemn obligation to labor for God; and I must go to India at any sacrifice. I owe something to my perishing fellow-men; I owe something to my Savior. He wept for men — he shed tears over Jerusalem.

'Did Christ o'er sinners weep?
And shall our cheeks be dry?'"

At this time her letters to Mr. Newell breathe forth the most devoted missionary spirit, and exhibit her firm determination to do her highest duty and discharge her great mission at any sacrifice — at the cost of separation, tears, and death. And required it, think you, no effort to bring her mind into this godlike state? Cost it no toil to discipline the heart to such sore trials? Most certainly it demanded toil and effort; and many a visit to the cross was made, and many a view of the bleeding Savior obtained, ere she could turn her back on home and all that the young heart holds dear in this life, to labor and die far away over the rolling sea.

And we doubt if any other motive can be found so powerful as this to move the Christian heart to obedience. There is an inexpressible efficacy in the cross to bring all the various opposing elements into subjection, and produce order in the place of discord and opposition. With the cross the early disciples went forth, not as the crusaders went, with the sacred symbol on banners, and badges, and weapons, but wearing the *spirit* of the cross like a garment, having its doctrines engraven on the heart, and inspired and quickened into life by its mysterious energy. It was the cross that induced the early disciples to brave danger and death to spread abroad the new faith. The martyr at the stake, amid the curling flames, was supported by it; the exile from home, banished to rude and savage wilds, loved it; the prisoner in his chains, confined and scourged, tortured and bleeding, turned to it, and found satisfaction for all his wrongs; the laborer for God, amid wild men who had no sympathy for his vocation, carried the cross, and fainted not in his anxious toil.

And such was the effect of the cross on the mind of Mrs. Newell. It sent her forth in all the love of womanhood, and sustained her until the close of life. It produced on her the impression that it made upon the dreamer Bunyan, who saw it as he was escaping from the city of destruction. He came to it with a heavy heart and a burdened soul; but as he saw it the burden fell and rolled into the sepulchre, and his load was gone. He gazed with rapture and delight; and the tears burst forth and flowed down his cheeks, and joy and holy satisfaction filled his soul.

Here is the great moving motive, one which is above all others, one that is more effective than all others; and by this our heroine was animated and cheered in her missionary work.

Up to the time of her departure for India, the mind of Miss Atwood continued to be exercised with contending feelings. At one time the sacrifice, the toil, the labor, and self-denial of a missionary life would rise up before her. She would feel how great the trial must be to leave all the endeared scenes of youth and childhood, and go forth to toil, and perhaps die, among strangers in a strange land. Dark visions would often flit before her; and she felt how terrible it must be to sicken and expire on shores where no mother's kind hand could lift her anguished head nor smooth her fevered pillow. But at other times her spirit soared above the toil and sorrow, and dwelt with rapture upon the bliss, of seeing some of the poor, degraded heathen females converted to Christ. The glory of the great enter prise presented itself; and she realized the blessedness of those who leave father and mother, brother and sister, houses and land, for the promotion of the kingdom of Christ. From these various struggles she came forth purified, dead to the world, and alive unto Christ. Any sacrifice she was willing to make, any toil endure. It was her meat and drink to do the will of God and accomplish his work. After a full investigation of all the privations and sacrifices of a missionary life, after a solemn and prayerful estimate of all that was to be left behind and all that would be gained, she formed her opinion and decided to go forth. A feeble woman, just out of childhood, she linked her fate with an unpopular and scorned enterprise, and cast in her lot with the dark-browed daughters of India.

We have seen grand enterprises commenced and carried on; we have seen our fellow-men gathering imperishable laurels; but never before did the world witness so grand a spectacle, with so high an object to be accomplished by mortals, as was given in the departure of Harriet Newell to teach the lessons of Jesus in distant lands. We consider the career of Napoleon a glorious one. We cannot look upon his successful marches and battles, however much we disapprove his course, without something of admiration mingled with our abhorrence. There was a gorgeous glory which gathered around the character of that emperor of blood which hides his errors and dazzles the eyes of the beholder. But the true glory which gathered over that little band of missionaries, as they left the snow-covered, ice-bound coast of America, to find homes and graves in distant India, far outshines all the glitter of pomp and imperial splendor which ever shed its rays upon the brilliant successes of the monarch of France, the conqueror of Europe.

True, they went forth alone. No weeping church followed them to the water side; no crowded shore sent up its wail, or echoed forth the fervent prayer; but in the homes of the people, in the heart of God, these holy men and women were remembered. Had that beautiful hymn been composed for them, it could not have been more appropriate; and as they stood upon the deck of the wave-washed Caravan, it must have been the sentiments of all their hearts.

"Scenes of sacred grace and pleasure,
Holy days and Sabbath bell,
Richest, brightest, sweetest treasure.
Can I say a last farewell?
Can I leave you,
Far in distant lands to dwell?

Yes, I hasten from you gladly —
From the scenes I loved so well;
Far away, ye billows, bear me;
Lovely, native land, farewell!
Pleased I leave thee,
Far in heathen lands to dwell.

> In the desert let me labor;
> On the mountain let me tell
> How he died — the blessed Savior —
> To redeem a world from hell;
> Let me hasten
> Far in heathen lands to dwell."

Miss Atwood was united in marriage to Mr Newell on the 9th of February, 1812; and on the 19th the Caravan set sail, as before stated. The voyage to Calcutta, though attended with many things to render it unpleasant to a feeble American woman, was not a severe one. The weather most of the time was pleasant; and only occasionally did the waves sweep across the decks of the vessel, or flow through the windows into the cabin. Mrs. Newell spent her time in writing letters to her American friends and preparing herself for her missionary work. She now had leisure to examine her own heart and descend into the hidden mysteries of her soul; she had ample space to view the past and form plans for the future; she could try her motives by the unerring word of God, and, by humble prayer and careful meditation, be enabled to acquire strength which should prove equal to her trials. The cabin of a wave-tossed vessel, the loneliness of a voyage across the deep-green ocean, a separation from earth's homes and earth's hearts, were all calculated to lift up the pious mind, and centre the soul's best affections upon pure and worthy objects. Whatever of care and sorrow she might have had, however much or however little of anxiety might have filled her bosom, such circumstances were sufficient to bring her faith to the most severe test.

The voyage must have been severe but healthy discipline, and doubtless from it was learned many a lesson of grace and duty. As the snow-covered hills of her own dear home disappeared; as the tall chimney at the entrance of the harbor, from which the nightly flame burned forth a beacon to the mariner to guide him amid the storm, was lost in the distance; as the first night came on and darkness gathered over the wide waste of waters; as deep shadows fell upon the form of the plunging ship, — the missionary cause must have presented itself in a new light, and, to some extent, have been clothed with sombre hues. And as time rolled on and the distance from home increased, that sacred call of God, that holy mission on which she was employed must have appealed more strongly to the Christ-like heart of our missionary sister. The vessel encountered storm and tempest, the usual inconveniences of a sea voyage were endured, and danger in a thousand threatening forms appeared; but the hand which formed the channels of the sea preserved his servants, and amid storm and darkness guided the vessel which bore them to homes and graves in the dark places of the earth.

On her passage, Mrs. Newell kept an interesting journal, not only of her own feelings, but also of the incidents that rendered the voyage pleasant or painful and checkered it with evil or good. And such incidents there are always. When on the ocean, far from land, for the first time, the dullest and most stupid mind cannot fail of being aroused to new and awful emotions. Man learns of God at such an hour, and finds new proof of his grandeur and glory in every dashing wave and every whistling blast. With but a single inch between him and a watery death, he gazes from his narrow deck upon the boundless expanse of tossing, foam-crested billows; while, as far as his eye can stretch, not a foot of land appears. His vessel may be on fire, she may fill with water, she may be riven by lightning; but there is no friendly sail to which wrecked man may fly and be safe. His ship will founder in mid ocean, while not a single form appears to lend the helping hand, and not an eye is seen flowing with tears of pity; nothing is heard but the moan of ocean; nothing is seen but the sweeping surge, as it passes on, leaving no track of the submerged vessel.

Confined in towns and cities, enclosed in walls of stone and brick, chained to the wheel of custom, the soul of man becomes contracted and dwarfed. All around are monuments of human skill, and every thing as little as the human mind. But when he steps beyond the crowds of life and embarks on the bosom of the ocean, he begins to see Divinity in its most awful forms. He realizes the insignificance of the creature and the majesty of the almighty Maker.

So felt Mrs. Newell, as she stood upon the deck of her vessel and gazed upon the wonders of the deep. Each wave, as it dashed against the sides of the brig or rolled across her decks, seemed impressed by the hand of God; and in these scenes she realized, more than ever before, the grandeur and glory of Jehovah. She saw him mirrored out in the starry canopy above her head, and in the liquid mountains which lifted up their forms, and anon sunk into peaceful rest beneath her feet.

On the 17th of June the Caravan reached Calcutta and anchored in the harbor. During the passage along the river the vessel was hailed by boatloads of naked natives, who brought on board cocoa nuts, bananas, and dates in great profusion; while others were seen on the banks reposing in the sun, or bathing in the waters of the Ganges, or diving beneath the surface for the shellfish which are found there; while beyond, the country was seen in all the beauty of verdure and delight, as ever and anon the Hindoo cottage and the white pagoda reared themselves amid the trees which grew upon the shoreside.

On the arrival of the missionaries at Calcutta,

they repaired to the residence of Dr. Carey, where they found Mr. Marshman and Mr. Ward, all of whom were connected with the English Baptist mission station at Serampore. By invitation of Dr. Carey they visited the station, and were treated with the greatest kindness. But their hopes of usefulness were destined to be blasted. The East India Company was opposed to all attempts to Christianize the natives, and threw all their influence against the divine cause of missions. As soon as the government became apprised of the object of Mr. Newell and his associates, orders were issued for them to leave the country immediately. After a vast deal of parleying with the civil powers, permission was obtained to reside at the Isle of France; and on the 4th of August, 1812, Mr. and Mrs. Newell took passage on board the Gillespie for that place. Sorrow and distress now began to roll upon them in deep, sweeping waves. The crew of the vessel were profane and irreligious, the weather boisterous and unpleasant; while the spirits of the missionaries themselves were at a low ebb. For some time no progress was made, and the frown of Providence seemed to rest upon them. What purpose God had in view in surrounding them with such trials, they knew not; but with humble faith in all his allotments they bore submissively, but sadly, this new trial of their devotion. The delicate state of Mrs. Newell's health rendered their sorrows doubly annoying to her sensitive and refined mind. She shrunk from a contact with the rude beings around her, and in the society of her husband alone found enjoyment; and even this was not free from interruption. The morning and evening prayer was disturbed by the profane jest or the blasphemous ribaldry of God-hating men, who viewed our missionaries as deluded fanatics, justly deserving the contempt of all. Even the respect due to the weaker sex was not wholly observed; and the pious woman was often compelled to listen to expressions which would have brought a blush to the cheek of the strong man. Sickness and sorrow found but little sympathy; and the days seemed long and tedious, even to one who had not learned to complain of the wise discipline of a Father's hand.

While on this voyage, about three weeks before their arrival at the place of destination, she gave birth to a daughter, and became a mother. The sweet infant lived but five days; "blushed into life and died." The day before its death, the rite of the church, by which the little stranger into this cold world was given to God, was performed. They called her by the mother's name, and watched over her until she breathed her last breath upon her mother's bosom, and then sunk the form into the cold waters of the deep. As the corpse was lowered down over the side of the vessel, holy voices sung the sweet and tender hymn,—

> "So fades the lovely, blooming flower,
> Frail, smiling solace of an hour;
> So soon our transient comforts fly,
> And pleasures only bloom to die."

Soon after the death of her babe, Mrs. Newell discovered symptoms of the malady which soon carried her to an untimely grave. From the first, she had no hope of recovery. Several of her friends had died of the same disease; and when it fastened itself upon her system, she knew that her time had come. The slow, wasting consumption was on her frame, and her days were nearly run out. But the approach of death she viewed with perfect composure. Though far from home, far from all the endeared scenes of youth, from the roof which sheltered her in infancy, from the mother whose gentle hand guided her up to womanhood, she was tranquil. Death was only a dark shadow, which retreated before her as she advanced, and left her standing in the light of a cloudless day.

While on her dying pillow she read through the book of Job, and derived from its hallowed counsels much divine support and comfort. While contemplating the sufferings of that godly man, her own trials dwindled away, and she lost sight of her own anguish in the deeper woes of another. Often did she ask, as she remembered what others had endured and thought what trials some had experienced, —

> "Shall I be carried to the skies
> On flowery beds of ease,
> While others fought to win the prize,
> And sailed through bloody seas?"

Sometimes she wondered why she should be thus early taken away. She had left home and friends to labor for God in a heathen land; and why at the very onset he should call her to the grave, she could not understand. The great desire of her heart was to be the humble instrument in the conversion of sinners. She wished to win souls to Christ — to turn the attention of the dying heathen to the saving cross. Hence, when she found that, ere her work had fairly commenced, she was to be summoned away to her reward, torn from the arms of her husband, and removed beyond the province of toil, she failed to read the purpose of her Maker. All was gloom, and in calm submission she bowed her head to the coming storm. What was dark now she hoped to understand when the secrets of all hearts are known, and trusted that God was able to glorify himself as much in her death as in her life.

During her sickness she gave expression to the feelings of her heart, and proved to all around her that death had lost dominion over her; that the grave had secured no victory; and when she met the terrors of one and the silence of the other, it was as the conqueror meets his smitten foe. Her last words were, "How long, O Lord, how long?" and with this sentence on her lips she passed away.

Mrs. Newell died on Monday, the 30th of November, 1812, at the Isle of France, leaving her husband to labor alone for the conversion of the heathen. After the death of his wife Mr. Newell removed to Ceylon, and from thence to Bombay, where, after laboring a few years and doing his Master's work in tears and sorrow, he went down to his grave on the 17th of May, 1821.

The scene now closes. We have followed a devoted servant of Christ from youth to womanhood — from early childhood to an early grave. It is pleasant to contemplate such an example, to shed tears of gratitude over such a tomb. The name we pronounce deserves to be recorded in a more conspicuous place in the book of fame than any name which has gathered gory laurels on the wet field of carnage; she deserves a higher monument than rises over the resting-place of earth's proudest conqueror — a monument not of marble, nor of brass, nor of gold, but one which shall lift its summit until a halo of eternal light shall gather about it and gild it with the beams of glory. And such a monument she has. When the clouds and mists of earth are dissipated we shall see it, sinking its base deep as the darkness of a world of heathenism, and lifting its summit high as the throne of God.

Harriet Newell was the great proto-martyr of

American missions. She fell wounded by death in the very vestibule of the sacred cause. Her memory belongs not to the body of men who sent her forth, not to the denomination to whose creed she had subscribed, but to the church — to the cause of missions. With the torch of Truth in her hand she led the way down into a valley of darkness, through which many have followed. Her work was short, her toil soon ended; but she fell, cheering, by her dying words and her high example, the missionaries of all coming time. She was the first, but not the only martyr. Heathen lands are dotted over with the graves of fallen Christians; missionary women sleep on almost every shore; and the bones of some are whitening in the fathomless depths of the ocean.

Never will the influence of the devoted woman whose life and death are here portrayed be estimated properly until the light of an eternal day shall shine on all the actions of men. We are to measure her glory, not by what she suffered, for others have suffered more than she did. But we must remember that she went out when the missionary enterprise was in its infancy — when even the best of men looked upon it with suspicion. The tide of opposition she dared to stem; and with no example, no predecessor from American shores, she went out to rend the veil of darkness which gathered over all the nations of the East.

Things have changed since then. Our missionaries go forth with the approval of all the good; and the odium which once attended such a life is swept away. It is to some extent a popular thing to be a missionary, although the work is still one of hardship and suffering. It is this fact which gathers such a splendor around the name of Harriet Newell, and invests her short, eventful life with such a charm. She went when no foot had trodden out the path, and was the first American missionary ever called to an eternal reward. While she slumbers in her grave, her name is mentioned with affection by a missionary church. And thus it should be. She has set us a glorious example; she has set an example to the church in every land and age; and her name will be mingled with the loved ones who are falling year by year; and if, when the glad millennium comes and the earth is converted to God, some crowns brighter than others shall be seen amid the throng of the ransomed, one of those crowns will be found upon the head of HARRIET NEWELL.

CHAPTER II.

ANN H. JUDSON,

OF BURMAH.

NOTORIETY is one thing, and true glory is quite another thing. Many persons have become notorious around whose lives no true glory or dignity has appeared; and many men have been honorable in the highest sense who have lived unknown to fame, and unheard of beyond a narrow boundary.

The world's estimate of glory is a false one. It attaches too much importance to physical force, to noisy pomp, to the glitter and show of conquest, and gives too little honor to the silent but majestic movements of moral heroes.

Had any body of men labored long and suffered much to save poor human life and draw from burning dwelling or sinking wreck some fellow-man, their deeds would be mentioned in every circle; humane societies would award them tokens of distinction and approbation; and they would be deemed worthy of exalted honor. Nor would it be wrong thus to give them praise. The man who risks his life to save another deserves a higher, prouder monument than ever lifted itself above the tombs of fallen warriors who on the gory field have slaughtered their thousands.

Nor will the deserved approbation of the great and good of earth long be withheld from the heralds of salvation on heathen shores. The majesty of the missionary enterprise is beginning to develop itself; success is crowning the toil of years; and heathendom is assuming a new aspect. Under the faithful labors of self-denying men, the wilderness is beginning to blossom as the rose. Here and there, amid the sands of the wide desert once parched by sin and consumed by the fiery blaze of heathenish cruelty, the plants of grace are beginning to appear, and Christian churches are springing up to spread themselves like green vines upon the broken ruins of demolished idols.

It is too late now in the world's history, too late in the progress of thought, to vindicate the course pursued by the two pioneer female missionaries. When the Caravan sailed down the harbor of the "City of Peace," there were enough to curl the lip and point the finger of scorn. The devoted messengers of Jesus were charged with indelicacy, with a false ambition, with a spirit of romance and adventure, with a desire for ease and gain. As time rolled on, all these charges were withdrawn; the characters, views, and feelings of these heroic women were raised above suspicion, and now they are enveloped in a flood of glory.

> "They left not home to cross the briny sea
> With the proud conqueror's ambitious aim,
> To wrong the guiltless, to enslave the free,
> And win a bloodstained wreath of dreadful fame
> By deeds unworthy of the Christian name."

Their errand was to carry mercy to the perishing and hope to the despairing; and in the name of their great Master they executed their high commission. Depending alone on God, and inspired by his grace, they labored on, amid all the doubts and sneers of others, until their holy lives and correct deportment challenged the approbation of the most sceptical, — until God honored their work by great success, — until men, hardened men, began to yield.

> "And by degrees the blessèd fruits were seen
> In many a contrite and converted heart,
> Fruits which might cause unbidden tears to start
> From eyes unused to weep; because they told
> Faith was their polar star, and God's word their guide."

And future ages will honor them. When the names of Mary and Elizabeth, of Joan of Arc with her wild enthusiasm, of De Staël and her literary contemporaries, have all been lost, these will live as fresh as ever.

Ann H. Judson was born at Bradford, December 22, 1789. She was the daughter of John and Rebecca Hasseltine, worthy inhabitants of that pleasant village. Her childhood was passed within sight of the house which contained the friends, and around which clustered the employments and pursuits, of Harriet Newell. With only a narrow river rolling between them, these two devoted servants of God passed through the period of youth, little thinking how their names and fortunes were to be linked together in the holy cause of human good. Like her beloved associate, Miss Hasseltine was early in life a pupil at Bradford Academy, and made commendable progress in her studies. There she was beloved by all. The teachers regarded her as an industrious, dutiful, and talented scholar; her associates looked upon her as a sincere, openhearted, cheerful companion. Unlike Mrs. Newell, who was sedate and grave, exhibiting a seriousness almost beyond her years, Miss Hasseltine was ardent, gay, and active. She loved amusement and pleasure, and was found seeking enjoyment in all the avenues of virtuous life. One of her schoolmates, speaking of her, says, "Where Ann is, no one can be gloomy or unhappy. Her cheerful countenance, her sweet smile, her happy disposition, her keen wit, her lively conduct, never rude nor boisterous, will dispel the shades of care and hang the smiles of summer upon the sorrows of the coldest heart." Her animation gave life to all around her, and made her, at school, an unusual favorite; at home, the joy of her father's dwelling. It was probably this cheerfulness of her natural disposition which in after years enabled her to endure such protracted sufferings, and, by the side of her missionary husband, smile amid clanking fetters and gloomy dungeons. She loved to look upon the bright side of every picture, and seldom spent an hour in tears over any imaginary sorrow. On the front of evils she generally discerned signs of good; and often, while others were in sorrow, her heart was glad. Her sedate parents looked upon these exhibitions of cheerful disposition with some feelings of regret, and often chided their child for what they deemed an uneasy and restless spirit, little thinking that this very cheerfulness was to sustain her under many a trial which would have bowed others to the earth with crushed and broken spirits. God seemed to have adapted her to the very position in which he designed to place her; and her whole after career gave evidence of the wisdom of the divine arrangement. Had she been of different mould, she would have sunk ere half her work was done, ere half her toils were over.

While at Bradford Academy, Miss Hasseltine became a subject of renewing grace. Her own account of her conversion, found in her published memoir and elsewhere, is of the deepest and most thrilling interest to every pious heart. During the first sixteen years of her life, she, according to her own statement, had few convictions. She had been taught that she must be moral and virtuous, and in this way avoid suffering and secure peace of conscience. The awful necessity of being "born again" did not press itself upon her attention. Light and vain amusements engrossed much of her time, and employed many hours which should have been given to God and the practice of holiness. The prayers which she learned in youth were now forgotten, her Bible neglected, and her mind given up to vain and sinful pleasure. She did not realize that she was immortal; that she was a traveller to a long and unknown eternity; but the present hour, the present moment, received all her care and engrossed all her attention. From this state she was aroused by seeing in a little volume which she took up to read on Sabbath morning, just before going to the house of God, this solemn sentence: "She that liveth in pleasure is dead while she liveth." The words sunk deep into her thoughtless heart. In vain she strove to banish them; but they would return upon her memory, and linger there with tormenting obstinacy. Vain was it that she mingled in scenes of gayety and mirth; vainly did she become "the gayest of the gay." The conviction became stronger, as each week rolled away, that she was *a lost sinner*. Under the influence of divine truth she continued to become more deeply impressed with the importance of giving her heart to God and being a new creature. She herself says, "I lost all relish for amusements; felt melancholy and dejected; and the solemn truth that I must obtain a new heart, or perish forever, lay with weight upon my mind." At length her feelings became so overpowering that she could not confine them within her own bosom. God had rolled such a weight of conviction on her mind that she was almost crushed to the earth. How God could forgive *her* sins, she could not see. How one so guilty, so rebellious, so hardened, could obtain mercy, she did not know. Instead, at this time, of giving her heart to God, she resorted to other means to find relief from sin. She gave up many of the comforts of life, locked herself into her room, and spent many weary hours in self-imposed penance. Against the holy claims of God her heart soon rebelled, and she longed to be taken out of her misery.

At length she attained a more scriptural view of the way of salvation; she saw Christ as a vicarious sacrifice, and felt that, if saved at all, it must be by his blood, and not by her own imperfect righteousness. This view of Jesus was sweet and precious. He had become, not the Savior of the world, but *her* own Savior; he had died, not merely for the sins of the race, but for *her* sins; and in this sacred contemplation her soul found sweet relief. The torturing load of fears was gone; one sight of Christ had changed the heart and taken away its grief and sin. Like a liberated slave she rejoiced in perfect freedom, and her happy soul went out in joyful thanks to Him who had wrought the work.

With a heart changed by God, she seemed to pass from rapture to rapture, from bliss to bliss. Beneath the operations of grace her mind and her heart seemed to be enlarged, and to a wonderful extent she drank in the truth of the inspired word. Doctrines which until now had been all shrouded in darkness were readily comprehended. The great plan of salvation by the cross excited her wonder and admiration, and she loved to dwell upon it as the way in which she herself had been saved. All the energy of her soul seemed to be aroused to action. She was in a new world, inspired by new hopes, living a new life, a new creature.

The character of Miss Hasseltine's mind may be inferred from the nature of the books which, at this period of her experience, she read with the greatest eagerness. Instead of resorting to works of a superficial cast for instruction, she selected the profound dissertations of our most learned theologians, and read with much interest, as we are informed by her biographer, "the works of Edwards, Hopkins, Bellamy, and Doddridge." In the investigation of the deep and awful things of God she spent much of her time, and, with a humble desire to know the truth and obey it, sought wisdom from on high.

On the 14th of September, 1806, Miss Hasseltine made a public profession of religion, and connected herself with the Congregational church in Bradford, and for the first time partook with the company of believers of the broken emblems of a Savior's infinite compassion. The observance of this ordinance was full of blessing; at the table, according to her own testimony, she renewed her covenant with her Maker, and more solemnly than ever gave herself to the holy work of God. She felt how needful the assistance of a higher power was to keep her from the snares into which young Christians are so liable to fall.

After leaving the academy, Miss H. engaged as a teacher, and with considerable success employed herself in her vocation, in Haverhill, Salem, and Newbury. Teaching with her was not an ordinary employment; she remembered that her pupils had souls as well as bodies; and while she was striving to expand the youthful mind, she also endeavored to improve the youthful heart, and impress upon the conscience those lessons of truth which time could never efface. It was at the same conference in which the acquaintance between Mr. and Mrs. Newell commenced that Mr. Judson was introduced to the subject of this sketch. He was then in need of a companion who would share his anxieties, his labors, and his sorrows; and he fixed upon Miss Hasseltine as the one whose tastes and feelings most accorded with his own. He was probably attracted by her ardent piety, her brilliant intellect and her joyous spirit. Having duly considered the subject, he gave her an invitation to go out with him to distant India, and be his companion in the brightest hour of his prosperity and in the darkest moment of his adversity. To decide the question was not an easy matter. It was connected with obligations which she did not hastily assume, and hence it was several months ere she had resolved to go. She was at times fearful that her disposition for what was in itself romantic and strange would bias her judgment and lead her to pursue a course which she should regret when too late to turn back. Hence she brought all her feelings and motives to a severe test, and looked down deeply into the hidden mystery of her heart. Before God she laid herself completely open, and sought, by humble supplication, his divine direction. With no example but that of Harriet Newell, who had just consecrated herself to the work, she decided to make India her home, and suffering and privation her lot. Her letters upon this subject, about this time, abound with passages of thrilling interest, and give evidence that the subject of missions absorbed her whole attention and pervaded her whole nature.

On the 5th of February, 1812, Mr. and Mrs. Judson were married at Bradford; on the 16th Mr. Judson and his associates were ordained in Salem, and on the 19th they sailed for Calcutta. While on the passage, a change occurred in the feelings and views of Mr. Judson which materially changed his whole course. He was aware that at Serampore the Baptists had established a mission station which was in successful operation. He knew that he should come in contact with the peculiar views of that denomination, and be under the necessity of replying to the objections which would be urged against his own sentiments. His own mind was at rest upon the subject; but he wished to be fully armed against all the arguments which he should meet on his arrival. To prepare himself for an encounter with Dr. Carey and his associates, he commenced the diligent study of the word of God and such works as he had in his possession. As he advanced in his investigation, doubts began to thicken around him; his mind, instead of being more fully convinced, began to waver; the arguments of Baptists he did not know how to overcome. Thus it continued for a while, until, a short time after their arrival, Mr. and Mrs. Judson threw aside their former views of baptism, and adopted the sentiments of another denomination. The particulars of this change are given by Mrs. Judson in a letter to her friends. By her we are informed that for a long time her husband's new notions did not correspond with her own. With woman's ingenuity and skill, she sought to dissuade him from any public statement, and even from an investigation of the subject. She well knew to what such a step would lead. The friends who had been so kind to her, who were then supporting her, who were willing still to support her, would be obliged to withdraw their aid. They could not, in conscience, support a missionary who was promulgating what they deemed an error, and consequently would recall her husband to America. Nor was this the worst. She had many personal friends who would be unable to appreciate her motives and understand her true position. They would be surprised, grieved, and perhaps offended. And to be encountered, was the odium of changing one's religious opinions, the charge of fickleness, and the consequent loss of reputation. Besides, the change, if made, would be a small one — simply a question of difference between the application to the body of a few drops of water and an entire immersion. This, to her mind, was a small change, which to her companion involved great consequences. Hence she endeavored to have him give up the subject and quiet his mind upon his previous opinions. Laughing, she told him, "if he became a Baptist, she would not." But the examination had been commenced, and could not be given up; and ere it was completed, she herself was a convert. That she was sincere, we have no room to doubt; by the change she had every thing to lose and nothing to gain. And it was made willingly, at

.ast; when her judgment was convinced, she hesitated not.

The brethren at Serampore knew nothing of the change of views until they received a letter from Mr. Judson, asking baptism at their hands. That it was to them an occasion of gladness, we need not state. Weary with toil, they received this addition to their number as a gift of God, sent at this time to stay up their hands and encourage their hearts. It gave them new strength to meet the tide of opposition and bear up under the heavy load of missionary care and anxiety.

They were baptized on the 6th day of September, in the Baptist chapel at Calcutta, and shortly after Mr. Judson gave his reasons for the change in a sermon which has already passed through several editions, and which is regarded by his friends as a conclusive argument.

Whatever may be the opinion in regard to the correctness of Mr. J.'s new views, — whatever may be the views entertained of the denomination to which he united himself, — no godly man will regret the result to which it has led. His change aroused to action the slumbering energies of the whole Baptist section of our Zion, inspired that sect throughout the land with a new and holy impulse, and originated the convention, which now, under the name of the Missionary Union, is doing so much for a dying world. But for the change of Judson's sentiments upon the question of baptism, a denomination which is now contributing nearly two hundred thousand dollars annually for missionary purposes might have stood aloof from the holy work for many years. The hand of God in this event is plainly seen — the hand of God, touching the heart of a mighty party, and animating it with a true, godlike missionary enthusiasm.

About the time of this change Mr. J. wrote a letter to Dr. Bolles, in which he threw himself upon the Baptists of America for support and sympathy. Previous to receiving a reply, he sailed with his companion for the Isle of France, at which place Mrs. Newell had been buried previous to their arrival. The desolate man met them on the shore, and with tearful eyes described to them the dying scene and the solitude of his own heart. Mr. Judson preached a while to the people and the soldiers who were stationed at the Isle of France, where he was the instrument of much good.

Providence did not favor his remaining at that place, and he left it for another field of labor, and at length, after many difficulties and hardships, arrived at Rangoon, in Burmah, in July, 1813. At this place several attempts had been made to establish a mission station, but all had failed; and the last missionary, a son of Dr. Carey, had departed a short time previous to the arrival of Mr. and Mrs. Judson.

Our missionaries repaired to the house which Mr. C. had formerly occupied, about half a mile from the town. Mrs. Judson, being feeble, was borne upon the shoulders of the natives; and as she passed along, or as the bearers stopped to rest, a crowd of people gathered around her. Some came to her side and looked under her bonnet, and retired with boisterous merriment. But all their little annoyances she suffered with patience, knowing that here she was to find a home, and to these very people declare the word of God.

The manner in which they acquired a knowledge of the language is somewhat novel. They were unable to find any one who was acquainted with the English language, and were obliged to select an agreeable and pleasant Burman, who, to the best of his ability, instructed them in the principles of the language of his country. They would point to houses, and trees, and the various objects around them, and he would give their names in Burman. Thus after a while they were able to make themselves understood, and, being willing learners, they very soon made rapid progress — rapid, considering the discouragements under which they labored — being without both grammar and dictionary, or any other book which could materially assist them. Slow and discouraging indeed, compared with the labor of learning some other languages under different circumstances, was their advancement; but when the circumstances under which they commenced and prosecuted the task of learning the language of the Burman nation are considered, we should imagine that almost any progress was rapid.

On the 11th of September, 1815, their first child was born. They gave him the name of Roger Williams, in honor of one of the greatest advocates of human liberty which the world has ever raised. Eight months they loved him and watched over him, at the expiration of which he sickened and died. He was buried in the garden of the mission house; and the tears of the weeping parents, and a small company of kindhearted but ignorant Burmans, watered the little grave, in the silence of which the infant had found repose.

For a few years after the arrival of Mr. Judson at Rangoon, the officers of government manifested towards the mission a friendly spirit. The missionaries were invited to visit the viceroy and vicereine at their royal residence, and received their visits in return. The mission was accomplishing the object of its establishment, and from time to time was reënforced. Even the bands of hostile robbers respected the property and persons of the men of God; and they fondly dreamed that it would thus continue.

In April, 1819, Mr. Judson commenced preaching the gospel in a building erected for the purpose, called a zayat. Until this time he had not attempted publicly to discourse after the manner of preaching in America. His audience consisted of twelve or fifteen adults, besides a large number of children. On the 27th of June, the first Burman convert was "buried with Christ by baptism." It was to the devoted Judson and his companions a day of pure and holy joy. The first fruits of their labors began to appear; and when Moung Nau went down into the water, a burst of gratitude went up from the deepest places of their hearts. The day was beautiful, the audience quiet and attentive, as there, beneath the very shadow of Gaudama, in the waters of a lake consecrated to the rites of heathenism, the new-born soul gave outward signs of the inward change. With what feelings of interest the missionary must have looked upon the first convert, we can only imagine. For that day he had waited and toiled for years; and as he pronounced the impressive formula, and in the name of the true God laid the dark son of India beneath the yielding waves, the feelings which rushed upon him must have been almost overpowering.

On the next Sabbath they sat down together at the communion table to celebrate the death of Christ — to commemorate the scene of Calvary. What a picture! The first offering of Burmah to the Lord; the first convert from that great empire, with his pale teacher, kneeling at the same altar, drinking of the same consecrated cup, and believing in "one Lord, one faith, one baptism." The second baptism was ministered on the same spot to two other converts. Amidst profound and holy stillness they descended into the water, where, a short time previous, Moung Nau had witnessed a good profession. The low and solemn tones of prayer were heard, the voice suppressed, in fear of arousing the ferocious enemy. There was no sermon, no address, no song; the record was on high, and angels looked down as spectators of the thrilling event. Around them, in earth's homes and in earth's hearts, there was no sympathy; but in heaven a chord was touched which will vibrate forever.

Shortly after the baptism of the two converts, opposition to the mission began to be manifested. Those who came to the mission house had evil in their hearts. To shield themselves from all harm, and secure the protection of the government, Mr. Judson and Mr. Coleman, who had been sent out in company with Mr. Wheelock a short time previous, determined to visit Ava and see the king. They did so, and with some difficulty obtained a hearing. They took with them the Bible, which was in six large volumes, decorated with gold, and well calculated to attract the attention of a heathen monarch. They were introduced into the palace and seated among the nobles. When the king appeared, the whole heathen throng prostrated themselves with their faces to the earth; the missionaries alone remained erect. After some conversation they presented their petition, and a tract on the being of God. The proud monarch read the petition through, and coldly handed it back to his minister. His eye then glanced over the little book; he read a single sentence, and then dashed it to the ground. Without ceremony they were hurried away from the palace, and, after various annoyances, were allowed to return to the friendly shelter of their boat. Sadly did they go back to the field of their labors to relate the story of their failure, and to toil on again until some new interruption.

Under the labors and sufferings incident to such a station, the health of Mrs. Judson began to fail rapidly, and it soon became evident that nothing but a visit to America would restore it. Consequently, in August, 1821, she started from Rangoon, and arrived in New York in September of the following year, spending some time in Calcutta and in England on her way. While in this country she accomplished a vast amount of good by her letters and conversation, and succeeded in inspiring the friends of missions with a deeper solicitude to see the heathen world converted to God.

In 1823, having regained her health, she returned to Burmah in company with Mr. and Mrs. Wade, who were sent out by the board to reënforce the mission. She arrived on the 5th of December, and found her husband in the midst of his toils and surrounded with disappointments and difficulties.

It soon become evident that Mrs. Judson had returned only to pass through scenes of unparalleled sufferings. On her arrival she found her husband about to leave for Ava, and immediately started with him. On the passage they encountered storms and dangers, and were, emphatically, in perils by sea and perils by land. While stopping at the town of Tsen-pyoo-kyon, about one hundred miles from the capital, they learned that the declaration of war had been made, and that the Burmans and English were at open hostilities. They reached Ava, and, without manifesting any fear or any interest in the hostile movements of the people, proceeded to build there a house and commence their operations. Soon the dreadful news came that the British had taken Rangoon. This catastrophe incensed the court at Ava, and Mr. Judson and Dr. Price were arrested as spies in the employ of England.

On the 8th of June, 1824, Mr. Judson was arrested at his own dinner table by a party of officers, led by an executioner whose power was absolute, and who held in his hand a black book, in which the names of his victims were recorded. With scarcely a moment's notice they threw him on the floor, and bound him with strong cords, and hurried him away. Mrs. Judson offered them money to release her husband; but they repulsed her with rudeness, and carried him, heedless of her tears and prayers, into the *death* prison, where he was loaded with three pairs of chains, and fastened to a long pole, to prevent the moving of his body.

In this trying situation Mrs. Judson returned, a lone, desolate woman, to her dwelling, and destroyed all her papers, journals, and writings of every description, lest they should be examined and found to contain something which would increase the sorrow of her husband. Her servants were taken from her and confined in stocks, and a guard placed about the house, who did their utmost to annoy and insult her. After some delay she procured permission to go abroad, and daily, at the prison gate, prayed that she might see the prisoners. Permission was at length given, and the fond wife sought her husband. She found his condition more deplorable than she had supposed. He was scarcely able to crawl to the door of his rude tenement; and while he stood in conference with the highminded and noble woman who had followed him beyond the seas, he was constantly annoyed by the suspicious and watchful keepers, who listened to their conversation and scrutinized every movement. So jealous were they, that, ere any arrangement could be made by which Mr. Judson's release might be effected, they were commanded to separate. In vain the wife urged her affection for her husband — in vain she appealed to manly feelings and love of home — in vain she exhibited the order of government by which she had been admitted — in vain she clung to the neck of her chained and suffering companion. No motive was strong enough to move the hard hearts of the cruel wretches, who seemed to take exquisite pleasure in the miseries of others. So completely does heathenism deaden the heart to all generous and elevated feelings that those strong men could witness unmoved, ay, with delight, the intense anguish of a feeble, weeping, broken-hearted woman. To every prayer she offered and every plea she made, they gave back words of cruelty and scorn; and when she entreated them, for the love of humanity, to allow her to converse with Mr. J. a few minutes longer, they refused; and as she hesitated, they cried, in angry tones, "*Depart, or we will drag you out.*"

The admirable conduct of this heroic woman, under such trying circumstances, we cannot too much applaud. Ceaselessly she labored for the release of her husband. From one member of the royal family to another she went, with prayers that they would intercede in her behalf. Repulsed every where, she fainted not, but toiled night and day for the accomplishment of her purpose.

After about a month's confinement, Mr. J. was violently beset with fever, and the governor gave orders that he should be removed to a more comfortable situation. He was accordingly placed in a little bamboo hut, and his wife permitted to attend him. Here he remained three days, when the English advancing upon the capital, the order was given for the removal of the prisoners. They were hurried away without warning, and Mrs. Judson was left in a state bordering on distraction. She soon found, on inquiry, the direction which the prisoners had taken. With a single servant and two Burman children, she started, with her babe, three months old, in her arms, to find her companions in suffering. She overtook them at Oung-pen-la, and found their condition to be wretched beyond description. Their journey was over a rough, burning road, and, chained two by two, they were whipped along like cattle bound to the place of slaughter. Their backs were blistered by the sun, and their feet scorched by the ground, until every step they took drew forth a groan of anguish, which their drivers answered with yells of delight. One poor creature fell in the pathway, and was dragged along until he expired.

To add to Mrs. Judson's distress, her assistant was taken with the small pox the morning after she arrived at Oung-pen-la; and soon her daughter Maria was reduced to the point of death by the same disease, and she herself was afflicted with the malady in a modified form.

The prisoners had been sent to this place that they might be burned in the old prison, in which, from the time of their arrival, they were confined, being chained together in pairs. But God had otherwise ordained: Judson was to live on. Soon an order for his release and return to Ava came; the government hoping he might be of service to them in their difficulties with the British. He was employed as interpreter and translator, and, as such, treated with some degree of kindness.

Wearied with continued anxiety, Mrs. Judson was prostrated by sickness soon after her return to Ava. Reason fled away; insanity took the place of calm and deliberate action; and for seventeen days she was a raving maniac. Absent from her husband, and dependent on the cold mercy of heathen women, she was indeed an object of pity. But from the borders of the grave she was raised up when all around thought her beyond the reach of hope. The hand of God reached down to the borders of the grave and rescued her from death, and placed her upon earth again, a fruitful laborer in the vineyard of her Master.

Time and space will not permit us to follow these devoted missionaries through all the suffering caused by this distressing war. Mr. Judson acted as mediator between the English and the Burmans, and by his ingenuity and skill, his eloquence and experience, saved a vast amount of bloodshed and crime. He was the instrument in securing the release of all the English and American prisoners who were confined in the dungeons of Ava, and restoring some from hopeless servitude to the friends and companions of youth. He conferred immense advantage on England, while he saved the capital of the vast Burman empire from fire and sword. To him, more than to any other man, is to be traced the amicable adjustment of the existing difficulties, and the settlement of the trouble on terms so favorable to the English residents of Ava.

One of the articles of the treaty then entered into provided that all the foreigners at Ava should have permission to leave unmolested. Mr. and Mrs. Judson availed themselves of this permission, and, on a beautiful evening in March, left with their fellow-workers and fellow-sufferers, and sailed down the Irrawaddy, bidding farewell to the golden city within whose walls they had suffered so much and been sustained by God so long.

Nor was Mr. Judson the only one who won praise and glory during that awful period. The companion of his toils was not idle. Her kindness to the prisoners — her arduous labors to do them good — her appeals to the government — her visits to the nobles — her ceaseless efforts — won for her undissembled gratitude and immortal renown. Nor are the acts of Mrs. Judson recorded alone on the records of Christian missions. The secular press of our own and other lands ascribed to her the honor of materially assisting in the adjustment of the existing difficulties, and, by her appeals and persuasions, doing much to prevent bloodshed and crime.

She went where no person of the other sex would have dared to go, and where, to any woman of less devotion and tireless perseverance, all entrance would have been denied. Though her husband, at this trying time, was the object of her peculiar care, yet she found time to do good to all the other prisoners. Like a ministering angel she moved among them, giving drink to the thirsty, food to the hungry, and clothing to the destitute.

A statement was drawn up by an English prisoner, and published in Calcutta and in England, in which the thanks of the prisoners are given to this estimable woman. The writer dwells upon the theme with the interest of one who has experienced acts of kindness and is himself under obligation. He ascribes to *her*, a feeble woman, the honor of having, under God, prepared the Burman empire to seek terms of reconciliation and peace. From a full heart he utters the tribute of his gratitude to the frail child of humanity who forgot her own weariness, forgot her own sufferings, forgot her own privations, sickness, and want, and sought out the wants of the victims of imperial despotism.

Her daily walk was from the prison to the palace. To one place she went to whisper words of kindness, to wipe away the tears of sorrow, to wet the parched lips of the dying with cool water, to bathe

the limbs bruised and chafed by heavy irons, and to apply healing balm to both body and spirit; the other place she visited to plead and argue with a proud court, and a haughty, tyrannical, and overbearing monarch. She risked her own life at every trial, but ceased not her perilous work until God crowned her labors with success — until the stubborn court of Ava relented — until she saw the fetters fall, and the prisoners again at liberty. The English nation owes her a debt of gratitude; for she has done more for it than many of its most illustrious warriors. Humanity is a debtor to her memory; for she was kind to man, and, in his want and suffering, surpassed humanity to do him good. Religion is her debtor; for she was one of its most devoted advocates, and presented in her life a sublime illustration of the power of faith. From Ava Mr. and Mrs. Judson removed to Amherst, a town which was founded at the close of the war in that territory, and which, by the treaty, was ceded to the English. It was at Amherst that Mrs. Judson was visited with the fatal fever which terminated her existence on the 24th of October, 1826.

At the time of her death Mr. Judson was absent from home, in company with Mr. Crawford, the British commissioner. Her sickness was short and painful. During most of the time her reason was dethroned; but in her moments of calmness she gave evidence that all was peace. Without the hand of her kind companion to lift her aching head, or bathe her throbbing temples, she died.

Mr. Judson returned, not to hear her voice, not to gaze upon her form, but to weep over her grave, and with his motherless child to sit in sorrow on the spot where she breathed her last. Such was the violence of her fever that she said but little, and left her husband without many of those tokens of kindness which surviving friends esteem of so much value.

They buried her at Amherst, under the shadow of a lofty hopia tree; and in that lonely grave her form now reposes, heedless of what is passing on the earth. Her child, which died shortly after she was buried, is laid by her side; and on the sacred spot the traveller often pauses to think of one of the most devoted and self-sacrificing women whose names have been mentioned with gratitude by the virtuous and the good. A marble slab, presented by the ladies of America, marks the grave, and points it out to every stranger.

Here we pause. Such labors, such self-sacrifice, such sufferings need no tongue to speak their merits. The worth of Mrs. Judson is engraved upon the hearts of all who claim the Christian character. For her works' sake she is beloved; and as long as the church endures, she will be remembered by all its members. Like Mrs. Newell, her fame belongs not to one sect or party, but to all who love our Lord and Savior Jesus Christ. Like her she went out when but few were ready to bid her " God speed " or bestow their money for her support.

On the record of American missions we find the name of no female who endured so much, who sacrificed so much, who accomplished so much. She fell not when the first notes of the great enterprise were ringing on her ears, but she made her grave amid the strife and confusion of the battle. She lived long enough to see the fruits of missions — to gaze upon the converts as they descended, one by one, into the baptismal wave — to see a door opened wide enough to admit laborers from every department of the Christian church. She mourned not, as did her sister martyr, that she was cut down ere she had labored for God and seen the happy result. They were born within sight of each other, in pleasant valleys, on the borders of the silvery stream. They met the companions of their missionary toils at the same time, and within a few days of each other decided to become the first heroines of the missionary church. Together they sailed — as precious a cargo as ever was tossed on the billowy sea. Together they landed on heathen soil, with high hopes of doing good. But, though united in their lives, they were divided in their deaths. Mrs. Judson lived on more than a half score of useful years beyond her companion; and if life is to be measured, not by the number of days and years, but by what is accomplished in it, or what is suffered during its lapse, then she lived ages — ay, ages of suffering, ages of labor, ages of virtue and piety — after Mrs. Newell had descended to her grave.

And where are they now? Go ask the angel throng, as they tune their harps to melodious songs on high, and they will point to two sister spirits, who day and night in company present themselves before God; and as one rank after another comes up from heathen lands to swell the chorus of the redeemed and ascribe their conversion to the efforts of the early missionary laborers who, under God, were made the humble instruments in the great work, meekly will be heard from the spirit lips of Harriet Newell and Ann H. Judson the reply, "Not unto us, not unto us, but unto the Lamb who was slain, but who liveth forever."

CHAPTER III.

ELIZABETH HERVEY,

OF BOMBAY.

IN the year 1812 a little company of missionaries sailed from the port of Boston for Bombay. They were sent out by the American Board to spread the knowledge of Jesus in the dark places of the earth. They founded their mission station — they labored long and cheerfully — they endured toil and self-denial — and saw the blessed results in the tokens of enlightened mind and regenerated heart.

On the evening of the first Sabbath in August, 1830, the windows of Park Street Church gave out a cheerful light; and he who entered saw congregated there an immense multitude of men and women. The pews, the aisles, the choir, were all filled, and deep interest was on all countenances and in all hearts. The occasion which drew this vast congregation was the setting apart of three young men, with their wives, to the solemn work of missions. William Ramsey, William Hervey, and Hollis Read were about to depart to "the land and shadow of death;" and the Christian community had come together to hear their voices, to see their countenances, for the last time. Soon broke over that crowd of human beings the well-known hymn, sung by a full choir and echoed by a responding people, —

> "Jesus shall reign where'er the sun
> Does his successive journeys run;
> His kingdom stretch from shore to shore,
> Till moons shall wax and wane no more."

Then was heard the solemn prayer of consecration, in which the missionaries were commended to God and to the word of his power; the blessing of Heaven was implored in their behalf; and to the care of Him who holds the winds, and who guides the dashing waves, the servants of God, the messengers of the church, were committed.

From the instructions given those beloved missionaries on that occasion we give the following extract: —

"The time has arrived to which you have looked with expectation and desire, when, with the partners of your lives, you are to bid farewell to your native land, and to enter upon a course of evangelical labors for the benefit of distant heathens.

"On such an occasion, it is obviously proper in

itself, as well as conformable to general usage, to address to you in public some considerations, in the form of advice and instructions, from those who have the superintendence of the mission with which you are to be connected. This is to you a solemn and eventful hour; and if, as we hope and believe, you have approached it with an earnest and truly benevolent desire to become heralds of divine mercy to your perishing fellow-men, it will be an hour always remembered with joy and gratitude in the future stages of your existence. If you partake of that holy, self-denying spirit which brought down the Son of God from heaven,— if you have any true sympathy with the apostles, who considered it as a great calamity to themselves if they were hindered in the work of preaching the gospel, — you will hereafter be able to say, with pure and indescribable delight, There was a period in our history when we publicly, in the house of God and in the presence of many Christian friends, devoted our lives to the service of Christ among the heathen. There was a time when the attachments to friends and country were dissolved, under the influence of that love which seeketh not its own, and which embraces, in its comprehensive regards, the suffering and the destitute of every clime.

"Congratulating you, therefore, on the possession of a temper which, if actually possessed, is of more value to you than all which this country or this world can furnish, we proceed to offer the following directions and remarks: —

"The vessel in which your passage is taken will, with the favor of Providence, convey you to Calcutta, where you will probably have the opportunity of conferring with some of those venerable men who led the way in the missionary enterprises of the last forty years. They are known and honored throughout the world; and honors will thicken and brighten around their memory long after the mere politician, statesman, and warrior shall have passed into oblivion.

"Without unnecessary loss of time, you will proceed to Bombay. Here a large and most interesting field invites your labor — interesting, not so much from any harvest which has been already gathered, nor because the precise period of ingathering can now be foreseen by human vision, as from the consideration that here the first mission of the Board was established; that here a noble and successful effort was made by our missionaries in pleading before governors the claims of the gospel; that here the first messengers of our churches cheerfully labored, till most of them have fallen asleep, their lives having been worn out by incessant exposure and toil; and, finally, that here preparations have been made for future labor, with a view to the wants of many millions, in whose language the message of salvation is delivered and the Scriptures are printed and circulated, while multitudes of children are trained up to read, reflect, and reason.

"The Christian community sends you forth, dear brethren, as messengers from our churches to the heathen. In the name of our churches we bid you *God speed.* The very act of our sending you forth in the name of the church implies that we hold ourselves bound to the same cause. By these public services we are solemnly pledged to regard you as a part of ourselves, not the less dear certainly because distant, your very distance being occasioned by your attachment to the common interests of the church. You have a just claim upon your Christian brethren in America for their prayers, their sympathies, and such a supply of your temporal necessities as will enable you to prosecute your great work. We are confident that, if all the members of our churches were convened in one place, they would unanimously sustain us in expressing these reciprocal obligations.

"Still, brethren, you must be sensible that the manner in which these pledges shall be redeemed will depend much upon the grace which is vouchsafed from above. If the spirit of piety should become low in our churches; if jealousy should divide their efforts; if professed Christians should generally become more entangled with this world, — the missionary enterprise of the country will be enfeebled. We would not distress you with apprehensions of this kind further than is requisite to call forth your earnest, constant, and importunate prayers that God would not leave our churches to a retrograde movement, which, in the present circumstances of the world, would be a most deplorable event.

"Confiding in that Savior who gave himself for the church and who loves it with an everlasting love, we affectionately commend you to his protection and blessing. When he, as the great Shepherd, shall gather his sheep into one fold, may you, and we, and multitudes of heathens saved by your instrumentality, be numbered among his chosen; and to him shall be glory everlasting."

The next morning the missionaries, with their wives, embarked on board the ship Corvo, for Calcutta. On the wharf the hymn was sung and the prayer offered; and the vessel swung off from the wharf amid the prayers and tears of the spectators. The vessel had a safe passage, and all the attention of Captain Spaulding was given to render the voyage pleasant and cheerful.

Mrs. Elizabeth Hervey, the wife of Rev. William Hervey, was born in Hadley, Massachusetts, and was the daughter of Deacon Jacob Smith, a beloved Christian and an estimable citizen.

During her early years she was remarkable for a prevailing desire to do good to others. Her young heart seemed set upon the work of benefiting her fellow-creatures; and she would make any sacrifice to confer happiness upon those around her. Though her heart had not been renewed and her mind made acquainted with the high and holy motives of the gospel, yet she recognized her obligations to others, and, while quite a child, endeavored faithfully to discharge them.

When she became a Christian, this desire to do good assumed a new and more divine form, and she exerted herself to lift up the race and adorn humanity. Her pastor, under whose ministry she was converted, says, "Doing good was her delight and her life. The subject of missions, years before she saw Mr. Hervey, was the great theme of her soul. She was alive to it at every point, and her memory will long be cherished here."

In the years 1815 and 1816 a sweet and gentle revival of religion was enjoyed in Hadley. Devoid of much of the excitement, the outward exhibitions of feeling, which such occasions bring, the living heart of the people was touched, and in all the homes of the inhabitants was felt and realized the heavenly results. In this revival Miss Smith became a child of God. Though amiable and outwardly virtuous, she became convinced that she needed a radical change such as she had never experienced. Still she made the sinner's excuse and fled to the sinner's refuge. One useless habit after another was given up, one sin abandoned, and one new step in virtue taken; but the wounded spirit found no rest. At length the cross appeared — the Savior's cross. She saw it — realized that by it she must be saved, if saved at all. With all a dying soul's deep earnestness she fled for safety and laid hold on the everlasting hope. The great salvation became her life, and in firm hope she embraced the Lord Jesus Christ.

In 1816 she united with the Congregational church in Hadley, and during her sojourn in this country maintained a consistent walk and conversation. She was emphatically a growing Christian — one who advanced in holiness, as the sun grows brighter when the day advances.

After her acquaintance with Mr. Hervey commenced, the question of a missionary life was laid out before her. She had often pondered upon it and prayed God to open the effectual door before her; and when the opportunity was presented, her heart warmly responded to the call from Heaven. That she had some trials and misgivings upon the subject cannot be doubted; but these were swallowed up in the desire to do good to her fellow-creatures. Though it required an effort to leave home and friends, she met the trial with unshaken firmness and devotion. Not long before they sailed for Bombay her husband preached a sermon, in which he gave expression to his own desires to promote the glory of God. In these expressions his heroic companion doubtless united; and though she could not publicly declare her own determination, doubtless her heart was united with his, not only in the social relations of life, but also in the firm and holy efforts for the elevation of our race. In that sermon, which we believe to have been the expression of the feelings of the fallen wife, Mr. Hervey says, —

"Besides the various objects in your own town and country which may have a claim on your charity, there are many millions of your fellow-creatures abroad who have a still stronger claim; stronger, because their woes are deeper and their wants greater. I stand now to plead the cause of Christ, not in behalf of the suffering bodies of a few poor saints at Jerusalem, but in behalf of the undying souls of six hundred millions of poor, benighted heathen. O for the eloquence of an angel, that I might exhibit to you the unsearchable riches of Christ, and the inconceivable miseries of men who are living and dying without a knowledge of him, in such a light that every one of you should weep because you have not a thousand fold more wealth to give, ten thousand hearts to pray, and twice ten thousand hands to labor for their salvation! I have no doubt that such would be your feelings, if you could now see things in the light in which you will see them shortly. You would then see that the end of living in this world, which was redeemed with the blood of the Son of God, and which is full of sinners perishing for want of that gospel which you possess, was something else than to heap together wealth to pamper 'the lusts of the flesh, the lusts of the eye, and the pride of life.' But the riches of Christ eternity will be too short to unfold; and I have neither time nor ability to present to your minds any thing like an adequate conception of the miseries of the heathen. That they are living and dying without the gospel, is enough to give every believer in the Bible an affecting sense of their wretchedness.

"I have told you the story of the Lamb of God — pointed you to what he left and what he submitted to in order to raise men to the riches of his everlasting love. He has gone back to heaven and taken his throne again; but he has left a cause on earth that is dear to him as the apple of his eye, and all the attributes of his name stand pledged for its final triumph. This cause he has intrusted, in a very important sense, to his disciples — beings in whose nature he came and suffered; and without their instrumentality it never did, and never will, go on.

"Thus he gives you all the privilege of being co-workers with him in saving the heathen. If you are not permitted to go in person to carry them the gospel, yet you may be perhaps equally useful by your prayers, and by furnishing the means for sending those who shall preach to them the unsearchable riches of Christ. If, then, you would elevate the degraded heathen to the purity of Christians, send them the gospel. If you would rescue them, not only from their present wretchedness, but from their darker prospects in the world to come, and inspire them with the high hopes of eternal salvation, send them the gospel. If you would see them at the last day on the right hand of the Son of man, and hear their bursting praises to God for your liberality and prayers, which helped to bring them there, now show how high you value their souls by contributing to send them the gospel, and by your fervent prayers that the blessing of the Lord may accompany your bounty and make it the means of their salvation.

"If other motives than those which have been presented were necessary to encourage you in this good work, I might prove to you that you will be the richer for every sacrifice you make to promote the cause of Christ; if not richer in temporal, yet certainly in spiritual blessings. I might say to you, in the language of Him who cannot lie, who holds the elements in his hand and can command them to spare or destroy your wealth, to bless or blast the work of your hands, 'The liberal soul shall be made fat; and he that watereth shall be watered also himself.' 'There is that scattereth, and yet increaseth; and there is that withholdeth more than is meet, but it tendeth to poverty.' Or, in the words of Him who gave up all his wealth and his life for us, 'It is more blessed to give than to receive.'

"I have chosen to rest the cause which the Lord has now permitted me to plead in his name mainly on the one great argument in the text; for in the whole compass of the universe there is not a motive to benevolent action so commanding as that. And I am persuaded it has not been presented to your minds in vain. No, I have been addressing those who know the grace of our Lord Jesus Christ; who feel thankful for that grace; and whose hearts burn within them to spread it abroad through the whole world.

"Is there one here who wishes to be excused from this work? Why, my brother, would you be excused? Look again. Is it no *privilege* to be allowed to do something to promote that cause for which patriarchs, prophets, apostles, and martyrs have prayed, and toiled, and died? Is it no *privilege* to help forward that cause which has engaged the hearts and hands of all the wise and good of every age? Is it no *privilege* to be associated with the choicest spirits now on earth in promoting the sublimest, the most benevolent, the most godlike cause that ever did or can employ the hearts and hands of men? Is it no privilege to labor, and pray, and give for the advancement of that cause which awakens the deepest interest in the bosoms of all the heavenly host, and which is the occasion of their loudest and loftiest songs of praise? Is it no privilege to do something for Him 'who left the highest throne in glory for the cross of deepest woe,' in order to give men a place in the mansions of his love? Is it no privilege to be a coworker with the blessed God in rescuing souls from a course of eternal sinning and suffering, and raising them to everlasting holiness and happiness and glory? Is it no privilege to aid in forwarding the only cause for which the world was made and for which all nature stands? The man who does not esteem it a high privilege that he may do something to promote such a cause may have the name, but cannot have the heart, of a Christian. If, then, any one desires it, let him be excused. The cause will go on. It has many friends, and is rapidly gaining more. It has Omnipotence for its support. Jesus 'shall have the heathen for his inheritance, and the uttermost parts of the earth for his possession.' He did not 'humble himself and become obedient unto death' for nought. 'He shall see of the travail of his soul and be satisfied.' 'All the ends of the earth shall see the salvation of our God.' 'The mouth of the Lord hath spoken it.'

"There is a mighty stir among the nations. The melting appeals from among the heathen have reached us from the four winds — ' Come over and help us.' The person who addresses you expects, in a short time, if the Lord will, to preach the unsearchable riches of Christ to some of these distant heathen He feels for the destitute in his own beloved land; but while he knows there are so many millions of immortal beings more destitute, — while he is to act under the commission, 'Go ye into all the world, and preach the gospel to every creature,' and while so few who are better qualified can think it their duty to these unhappy beings, — he feels that 'woe will be unto him if he preaches not the gospel unto them!'"

Inspired with such feelings, and cherishing such views, our sister went out to declare the love of God on heathen soil. Like those who before her had devoted themselves to the service of the Savior, she went forth not knowing whither she went or through what scenes she would be called to pass.

But God in his divine providence was soon to call her home to glory; her work was to be short, and her course quickly run. A few months only was she permitted to do good as she desired ere death called her away to the rest beyond the grave. She fell an early victim to her own self-sacrificing disposition. Shortly after her arrival at Bombay she was prostrated by the dysentery, which terminated her labors and her sorrows on the 3d of May, 1831.

Her lonely husband, writing to the father of his deceased companion, gives the following account of her dying hours: —

"Before this reaches you I trust you will have heard of the goodness of the Lord in bearing us safely over all the dangers of the Atlantic and Indian Seas, in providing us friends in Calcutta who spared no pains to make our stay in that city agreeable and happy, and in bringing us in safety to this, the destined field of our labors, our disappointments, our difficulties, and, as we expected when we left the shores of our native land, of our deaths. And although, since our arrival here, his afflicting hand has been laid heavily upon me, still I would speak only of his goodness. For when he afflicts and chastens his children, it is in loving kindness and tender mercy. It is not for his pleasure, but for their profit, that they may be partakers of his holiness. But if he has been good to me, he has been doubly so to your and my dear Elizabeth. Yes, God has made all his goodness to pass before her; for he has released her from all her sins and sufferings, and taken her to himself. 'O,' said she, 'how will the intelligence rend the hearts of my dear parents and sisters!' She paused a moment, and then added, 'But they will be supported. They know where to look for consolation.' Weep with me, my dear, dear parents, a little moment, and then we will together review the painful but merciful scene of her last sufferings.

"All that I have said above shows only the afflicting hand of God in this dispensation, which has snatched from me thus early the dear companion of my wanderings and toils, the tender partner of my joys and sorrows, the beloved wife of my heart; but in what remains to be said, will be seen his hand of *goodness* and *mercy*. In all her sufferings she was never heard to utter a single murmur or complaint, but was continually magnifying the goodness of the Lord. 'I did hope,' said she, 'that I should be permitted to do something towards elevating the miserable and degraded females of India to a state of refinement and happiness; but since God decides otherwise, his will be done. In this great conflict, some must fall as soon as they enter the field.' She repeated more than once a sentence which Dr Woodbridge dropped in his address to her on the evening of our marriage, in substance as follows: 'If we hear that, like Harriet Newell, you have fallen a victim to the climate of India even before you have commenced your labors there, still we say to you, Go.' 'Now,' said she, 'tell my friends, tell my beloved pastor, tell the dear church in Hadley, that I do not, and never have for a moment regretted that I came here. No; had I foreseen this hour, and all I have endured since I left America, I should have decided just as I did, if the path of duty had been as plain as it appeared to be.' During her sickness she often spoke of the love she felt towards the people of God. She was affected to tears at the kindness of her physicians and others who attended her. She addressed the members of the mission who called to see her on the importance of living to God

and of being faithful in his service. She expressed
an earnest desire that God would make her death
the means of a revival of religion in all the members
of the mission; and said, if such should be the case,
she should consider her early removal a greater blessing to the mission and to India than many years of
her poor service could be. The day before she died
she requested me to read to her the twelfth chapter of
Isaiah. 'Yes,' said she with emphasis, 'God is my
salvation.' As I read along she repeated after me
the third verse, emphasizing the word 'wells' —
'with joy shall ye draw water out of the *wells* of
salvation.' Some time afterward she wished me to
read the fourteenth chapter of John, which she said
afforded her much comfort. She repeated from
time to time many striking texts of Scripture and
parts of hymns, which, as I could leave her only for
a moment, I did not write down. Twice she repeated, and seemed to feel the full force of, that
beautiful and sublime stanza of Watts, —

> ' Jesus can make a dying bed
> Feel soft as downy pillows are;
> While on his breast I lean my head,
> And breathe my life out sweetly there.'

" One who stood near her said, ' O Death, where
is thy sting? O Grave, where is thy victory? The
sting of death is sin, and the strength of sin is the
'aw.' With animation she exclaimed, in addition,

' But thanks be to God, which giveth us the victory through our Lord Jesus Christ.' Mr. Allen said he hoped the Savior would be with her as she walked through the dark valley of the shadow of death. 'If this,' she said, 'is the dark valley, it has not a dark spot in it — all is *light*, LIGHT.'

"I said to her, ' My dear, your sufferings are great.' 'Don't,' said she, 'don't mention them; they have been nothing — nothing.' After a severe spasm, that seemed to convulse her whole frame, she exclaimed, ' O the pains, the groans, the dying strife! The spirit seems to be struggling and fluttering to get free from this cumbersome body.' She had, during most of her sickness, bright views of the perfections of God. ' His awful holiness,' she said, ' appeared the most lovely of all his attributes.' At one time she said she wanted words to express her views of the majesty and glory of Christ. ' It seems,' she said, 'that if all other glory were annihilated, and nothing left but his lone self, it would be enough — it would be a universe of glory.'

"The day before her death she was asked if she wished to see her child. ' Not now,' said she; ' I am too much exhausted. I fear it would overcome me. I will see him by and by.' After she had rested a while, she said now she would see the babe It was brought into the room. ' Let my husband,' she said, ' bring him to me.' I carried the child to her. She took it in one arm, and with the other embraced my neck. After a moment she looked up to the spectators with a smile, and said, 'Here is my family — my treasure — my earthly all. I cheerfully resign them into the hands of God.' On the morning of the day she expired I asked if she wished to send any particular message to any of her friends. She replied she did, and asked me to write what she dictated.

"Thus, my dear parents, I have finished the account of our beloved Elizabeth's last pains and joys in the flesh. Who can wish her back to earth? If any other one has reason to cherish such a wish, I have more. But severe as the stroke is upon me, I rejoice that her conflict with sin and suffering is over, and she is with her Redeemer. To know that she departed thus, triumphing in God her Savior, must afford you, as it does me, great consolation in the midst of the affliction which the news of her death will produce. But you, who knew her amiable disposition, her humble, prayerful, self-denying, holy life, have a better testimony that it is well with her now, than her dying deportment, whatever it might be, could give. She lived unto the Lord, she died unto the Lord; and there can be no doubt that she is now the Lord's.

"Last Sabbath evening Rev. Mr. Allen preached a sermon in the chapel, on the occasion of her death, from Romans xiv. 8. Since then I have learned that one careless man appears to have been awakened by the account that was given of her peaceful and triumphant death. Perhaps her prayers are about to be answered in a revival of religion here. The Lord grant that it may be so!"

When a beloved fellow-laborer dies at home; when the place of some dear one is vacated by death; when the hand of labor ceases to move and the heart of sympathy ceases to beat, — all around are saddened by the event: gloom covers the weeping church, and all who knew the fallen one bend in tearful silence over the grave. But when a missionary dies we can form no opinion of the feelings of those who are left in sorrow. Away from home and all the endeared scenes of early life, they become more strongly and firmly attached to each other. Between the members of the little band are formed the most tender ties, the most hallowed relations; and when *one* only departs, all hearts grieve and bleed as if the dearest earthly object had been removed.

Mrs. Hervey was buried near the scene of her labors — on heathen soil. The solemn funeral service and the pang of death were calculated to deepen the impression upon the minds of the converted and unconverted people; and the hymn, as it sent its mournful echo along the borders of the field of graves and sounded like the song of an angel amid the homes of the living, turned many a thought forward to that haven where the saint shall break from the repose of death, and come forth to the resurrection of the just, a new and glorified form.

> " Why do we mourn departing friends,
> Or shake at death's alarms?
> 'Tis but the voice that Jesus sends
> To call them to his arms."

Did we not have implicit confidence in the ways of God and in his special providence, — did we not feel that he is too wise to err, too good to be unkind, — our hearts would often faint as we hear of our devoted missionaries falling into the grave ere they have been permitted to labor to any considerable degree for the conversion of the heathen. Did we not feel perfectly satisfied in relation to the wisdom and mercy of the great Head of the church, we might well fold our hands and ask, " Will God be angry forever?" But who does not know that Jehovah is able to accomplish more by our deaths than *we* are able to accomplish by our lives? Who does not know that, from the very ashes of the tomb, he can send up a voice which will echo amid the shades of night and thrill the cold hearts of degraded men?

They who despond, as the tidings of woe come borne to us on almost every breeze which sweeps across the ocean, have lost sight of Him who holds in his hand the issues of life and the awful realities of death. These have drawn their eyes from the immutable promises and the ever-present Helper, and fixed them on the tomb, and the corpse, and the pale mementoes of mortality. They have ceased to reason like Christian men, and look at God's providence through the misty vision of scepticism and doubt.

Men admit that certain laws control the world of planets, the world of animal life, the world of intellect and reason; but seem not to have the idea that the providences are all under God's control, and regulated by fixed and certain laws. The sparrow that flits from bush to tree, and the mighty angel that wheels in everlasting circles around God's throne, are alike under divine protection. The feeblest insect which creeps upon the earth, and the highest archangel which ministers to God above, are equally safe beneath the divine protection. The Being who holds the universe, who keeps worlds in their places, is also employed to count the feathers of the young raven's wing, and number the hairs which cluster upon the human head.

Nor will God allow the places of the dead to remain long vacant. The conversion of the world is in accordance with his unalterable will and purpose; it was an article in the grand treaty of Calvary; and by all that God is has he pledged himself to give "the heathen to his Son for an inheritance, and the uttermost parts of the earth for a possession." Hence when, in the accomplishment of his grand design, one after another who went forth with high hope and joyful expectation is cut down, we may expect to see others raised up ready to accomplish greater good than their fallen predecessors.

The hearts of men are in Jehovah's hand. He moves upon the mind as he will, and takes those whom we least expect to lead on his hosts to the victory over sin.

Years ago the question was, "Who will go?" but now the question is being asked, "Who will stay at home and let *me* go?" "Who will resign his place in the missionary ranks, and let us go forth to do battle for the truth?" And we may expect this spirit to increase, until it shall be deemed the highest glory of the Christian minister to be a missionary of the cross of Christ.

Thanks be to God, the Church is arousing herself to her high duty, and already many have gone forth. The places of Harriet Newell, of Ann H. Judson, of Sarah D. Comstock, of Harriet B. Stewart, of Sarah L. Smith, of Elizabeth Hervey, of Henrietta Shuck, of Sarah B. Judson, and of others who are now quietly sleeping the long sleep of death, are filled. Others as faithful have come on to do the work which they left unfinished, and to stand around the moral plants which they began to cultivate.

And thus it will continue. When the faithful, laborious, successful missionary women who are now the admiration of the church and the world fall beneath the pressure of disease, toil, and time, a missionary Church will send out her daughters, who are reposing at home, to take the places of those who depart; and never will Burmah, Syria, Ceylon, Turkey, and other dark places be deserted, until over all the earth shall echo the song of the ransomed and the jubilee of the redeemed.

CHAPTER IV.

HARRIET B. STEWART,

OF THE SANDWICH ISLANDS.

HARRIET BRADFORD STEWART labored as a missionary at the Sandwich Islands. Amid this beautiful cluster of green spots in the bosom of the sea her efforts for human good were put forth; and here was the scene of her success, though not of her death.

The origin of the mission to the Sandwich Islands is somewhat peculiar. In 1809 two little boys shipped themselves on board of an American vessel bound for New York. They arrived at the great city, and, after residing there awhile, were taken to New Haven, Connecticut. They were fatherless, motherless children, with none to care for them; and their destitute, helpless condition soon drew the attention and won the sympathy of the Christian public. In a short time one of these youths was converted to God. Opukakia became a believer in the religion of Christ, and to the believers of our own land gave evidence of having passed from death unto life. Interest in these boys soon led to solemn inquiry into the condition of their country. This inquiry resulted in the establishment of a school for the instruction of heathen youth who were found in our land; and of the privileges of this school these two boys gladly availed themselves.

Shortly after they were taken to Andover and made acquainted with a class of young men who were about to graduate and go forth as heralds of salvation. Two members of that class soon determined on a missionary life, and selected these islands as the field of their labors. These young men were Hiram Bingham, and his classmate, Mr. Thurston. Their services were offered to the Board, and in 1819 were accepted. They were ordained at Goshen, Connecticut, and, under very solemn and impressive services, set apart to the work of the ministry.

On the 15th of October, 1819, in the vestry of Park Street Church, in Boston, they, with others, were organized into a church of the Lord Jesus. On the 23d of October this church set sail for the place of its destination — to the field of labor in which it was to thrive and flourish. Solemn was the scene, as on the wharf stood a company of beloved ones, who were leaving home and all the dear associations of youth for a barbarous nation. There, beneath the cool breath of autumn, they united in singing, —

> "When shall we all meet again?
> When shall we all meet again?
> Oft shall wearied love retire,
> Oft shall glowing hope expire,
> Oft shall death and sorrow reign,
> Ere we all shall meet again."

The voyagers were commended to the "God of ocean and storm" by Rev. Dr. Worcester; the apostolic benediction was pronounced; and the vessel gayly pursued her way down the harbor, and was soon lost from sight.

After the usual pleasures and annoyances of "a life on the ocean wave," the company were made glad by beholding in the distance the green hills of the islands on the soil of which they were to labor and pray. They found the people, not as Judson and Newell found those to whom they were sent with the torch of truth, but ready to believe and embrace the gospel. The messengers they sent ashore were greeted with shouts of joy, and their wondering eyes turned to consuming idols and demolished temples. They found a nation without a religion, a government without a church, a court without an ecclesiastic. The people seemed sunk in barbarism. They had no schools, no books, no pens, no means of information. Gross darkness was over all the people, and the land was enveloped in appalling gloom.

Undismayed by the gross ignorance and encouraged by the abolition of idolatry, the servants of God went to work. They distributed themselves through the islands, and every where preached Jesus and the cross. The effects of their labors were so apparent that the American Board were encouraged to send out repeated reënforcements; and in the progress of time Mr. Stewart and his accomplished companion arrived at Hawaii on their sacred mission. Perhaps there is no mission station on the globe, no scene of missionary toil, where such glorious results have been accomplished, and such wonderful changes wrought, as at the Sandwich Islands. Mr. Bingham, speaking of the condition of the people at the time of his arrival among them, says, " The nation had, on our arrival, neither books, pen, nor pencil, for amusement or business, or for acquiring information or communicating thought. They sat, like Turks or tailors, on mats spread on the ground; dipped their fingers in the dish to eat their fish, poi, and dog flesh, without knife, fork, or spoon. They stretched themselves at full length on the mats to play cards or otherwise kill time. Their water they drank from a gourd shell; and *awa*, the juice of a narcotic root, chewed by others and mixed with water in the chewers' mouths, they drank, as their fathers had done, from a cocoa-nut shell, for the same purpose that other intoxicating drinks and liquors are taken."

That the nobles as well as the common people were thus degraded and uncivilized, we are referred to a description, given by the same writer, of the king, who, with the royal family, was invited on board the vessel which conveyed out the missionaries. "They came off in their double canoes, with waving *kahalis* and a retinue of attendants. His majesty, according to the taste of the times, having a *malo*, or narrow girdle, around his waist, a green silken scarf over his shoulders, instead of coat, vest, and linen, a string of beads on his otherwise naked neck, and a feather wreath, or corona, on his head, — to say nothing of his being destitute of hat, gloves, shoes, stockings, and pants, — was introduced to the first company of white women whom he ever saw."

But the speedy change from drunkenness to sobriety, from ignorance to comparative intelligence, from theft and falsehood to honesty and truth, from shameless indecency to purity and chastity, from the violation of the whole ten commandments to the sacred observance of these ten, from barbarism to civilization and refinement, from brutish idolatry to the holy service of God, was astonishing even to those through whose instrumentality it was brought about.

Thirty years ago there was no church, no school house, no seminary of learning, no regard for the Sabbath, no thought of the great Jehovah: now all of these are found. The church tower lifts itself to heaven; the school and the seminary are sending abroad their instructions; the Sabbath is regarded by the mass of the people; and Jehovah is worshipped in spirit and in truth by thousands. During the year 1840 there were four thousand one hundred and seventy-nine additions to the church in the five islands; and since then conversions have been multiplied and converts have increased. The Bible has been printed, and edition after edition given to the perishing inhabitants, until thousands of them are rejoicing in the hope which it inspires. The whole temporal and spiritual condition of the people has changed. Christianity has made men of beasts, and lifted up the whole government in the scale of being.

Perhaps we can convey no better idea of the change which a few years' labor produced in the Sandwich Islands than by giving an extract of a letter, written by Rev. C. S. Stewart about the time of the death of his wife. It is a beautiful and thrilling description of a Sabbath in an island where, a few years before, was nothing but idol worship, heathen rites and ceremonies, and ignorant superstitions.

"At an early hour of the morning, even before we had taken our breakfast on board ship, a single person here and there, or a group of three or four, enveloped in their large mantles of various hues, might be seen wending their way among the groves fringing the bay on the east, or descending from the hills and ravines on the north towards the chapel; and by degrees their numbers increased, till in a short time every path along the beach and over the uplands presented an almost unbroken procession of both sexes and of every age, all pressing to the house of God.

"Even to myself it was a sight of surprise; not at the magnitude of the population, but that the object for which they were evidently assembling should bring together so great a multitude, when at this very place, only four years ago, the known wishes and example of chiefs of high authority, the daily persuasions of the teachers, added to motives of curiosity and novelty, could scarce induce a hundred of the inhabitants to give an irregular attendance on the services of the sanctuary. But now, —

> 'Like mountain torrents pouring to the main,
> From every glen a living stream came forth:
> From every hill in crowds they hasten down
> To worship Him who deigns in humblest fane,
> On wildest shore, to meet the upright in heart.'

"The scene, as looked on from our ship, in the stillness of a brightly-gleaming Sabbath morning, was well calculated, with its associations, to prepare the mind for strong impressions on a nearer view, when the conclusion of our own public worship should allow us to go on shore. Mr. Goodrich had apprised us that he found it expedient to hold the services of the Sabbath, usually attended at all the other stations at nine o'clock in the morning and at four in the afternoon, both in the fore part of the day, that all might have the benefit of two sermons and yet reach home before nightfall; for

> 'Numbers dwelt remote,
> And first must traverse many a weary mile
> To reach the altar of the God they love.'

"It was near twelve o'clock when we went on shore. Though the services had commenced when we landed, large numbers were seen circling the doors without; but, as we afterward found, from the impossibility of obtaining places within. The house is an immense structure, capable of containing many thousands, every part of which was filled except a small area in front of the pulpit, where seats were reserved for us, and to which we made our way in slow and tedious procession, from the difficulty of finding a spot even to place our footsteps without treading on the limbs of the people, seated on their feet as closely almost as they could be stowed.

"As we entered, Mr. G. paused in his sermon till we could be seated. I ascended the pulpit beside him, from which I had a full view of the congregation. The suspense of attention in the people was only of momentary duration, notwithstanding the entire novelty of the laced coats, cocked hats, and other appendages of naval uniform. I can scarce describe the emotions experienced in glancing an eye over the immense number, seated so thickly on the matted floor as to seem literally one mass of heads, covering an area of more than nine thousand square feet. The sight was most striking, and soon became, not only to myself, but to some of my fellow-officers, deeply affecting.

"With the exception of the inferior chiefs having charge of the district and their dependants, of two or three native members of the church and of the mission family, scarce one of the whole multitude was in any other than the native dress — the *maro*, the *kihee*, and the simple *tapa*, of their primitive state. In this respect, and in the attitude of sitting, the assembly was purely pagan; totally unlike those of the Society Islands; as unlike as to one at home. But the breathless silence, the eager attention, the half-suppressed sigh, the tear, the various feeling — sad, peaceful, joyous — discoverable in the faces of many, all spoke the presence of an invisible but omnipotent Power — the Power that can alone melt and renew the heart of man, even as it alone brought it first into existence."

Turning from the changes which have been wrought in these islands, — on which we have, perhaps, lingered too long already, — we turn to one through whose efforts a part of this work has been accomplished.

Harriet B. Tiffany was a native of Stamford, Connecticut. She was born on the 24th day of June, 1798. Her parents were honorably descended from an illustrious line, and Harriet inherited many of the noble qualities of her ancestors. Her youth was passed mostly in Stamford, Albany, and Cooperstown, in which places she endeared herself by many acts of kindness to all who knew her, and grew up to womanhood cherished and loved by all who came within the circle of her influence. In 1819 she passed through that mysterious change which is denominated regeneration. Repeated afflictions, the death of friends, and her own sickness led her to feel the need of a strong arm and a firm hope. Feeling the emptiness of earth, the vanity of human life, even in its best estate, she turned to Him who can give support to the soul in the hours of its dark night and guide it amid the gloom. By faith she saw the crucified One, and rested her sorrows and griefs on Him who was able to bear them. She was changed from darkness to light, from sin to holiness, from death to life.

The great subject of a missionary life was presented to her view, connected with a proposal to accompany Rev. C. S. Stewart to the Sandwich Islands as his assistant and companion. With trembling anxiety she submitted the case to the wise discretion of her Father in heaven: on earth she had none. As may be supposed, it was no easy thing for a young lady of high and honorable connections, who had always been surrounded with friends and educated in the circle of refinement and luxury, to leave all these. There were tender ties to be riven, fond associations to be broken up, dear friends to part with, and a loved home to leave behind; and when the momentous question was brought distinctly before her mind, it required a strong faith, a firm dependence on God, an entire submission to his will to induce her to take the solemn and important step; but, believing herself called upon by God, she decided in his favor, and lost sight of the sacrifice and self-denial of the undertaking.

She resolved to go — to go, though home was to be abandoned, friends to be left, loved scenes deserted, and a life of toil to be endured. She resolved to go — to go, though she might pass through a sea of tears, and at last leave her enfeebled body upon a couch that would have no kind friends to surround it when she died. She resolved to go, though she should find in savage lands a lowly grave.

She was married to Mr. Stewart, in the city of Albany, on the 3d of June, 1822. Mr. Stewart had already been appointed as a missionary, and was to go out to the Sandwich Islands under the care of the American Board. They sailed in company with a large number of others who were destined for the same laborious but delightful service. The sun of the 19th of November went down on many homes from which glad spirits had departed on their errand of mercy to a dying world; and on that day the eye of many a parent gazed upon the form of the child for the last time. Nor could a vessel leave our shores, having on her decks nearly thirty missionaries, without being followed by the prayers of more than the relatives of those who had departed. There was mingled joy and sorrow throughout the churches of New England, as the gales of winter wafted the gospel-freighted vessel to her distant destination.

They arrived, in April of the following year, at Honolulu; and, after a residence of a few days, located themselves at Lahaina, a town containing about twenty-five thousand inhabitants, who were mostly in a degraded condition. Here they found but few of the conveniences of life, and were obliged to live in little huts, which afforded but slight shelter from the scorching heat or the pelting rain. In these miserable tenements did the child of luxury and wealth reside, and in perfect contentment perform the duties of her station. She suffered, but did not complain; she labored hard, but was not weary; and, cheerful in her lot, smiled even at her privations and sorrows.

In 1825 her health began to fail. Unable longer to labor for her perishing heathen sisters, she sailed for England in order to enjoy medical advice and care; but instead of improving by the voyage, she continued to decline, until the hopelessness of her case became apparent. She embarked for America in July, 1826, her residence of a few months in England having rendered her no permanent benefit. In her low state the voyage was any thing but agreeable; and she arrived among her friends the mere shadow of what she was when, a few years before, she had gone forth in the flush of youth and the vigor of health.

For a time after her arrival strong hopes were cherished that she might recover. The balmy breezes of her own native valley, the kind congratulations of friends, the interest and excitement of a return to the scenes of youth gave color to her cheek and life to her step. But in the early part of 1830 the prospect of returning health was dashed, and Death appeared in all his terror. Long was her last sickness — so long that she groaned to depart and be with Christ. For many months she suffered and struggled on a weary bed, until the spirit call was heard, and golden gates were opened, and the ransomed one entered in. During this sickness she was sustained by the grace of God. Death found her ready, and led a *willing* victim down into the sepulchre, who exclaimed, as she entered it, " O Death, where is thy sting? O Grave, where is thy victory?"

Racked with pain and tortured by disease she murmured not, but, as each new cup of sorrow was put to her lips, meekly replied, " The cup which my Father hath mingled, shall I not drink it?" She was a remarkable instance of Christian submission and resignation under sufferings, and left behind her, to surviving friends, the joyful evidence that she had passed away to rest.

> " Spirit, leave thy house of clay ;
>   Lingering dust, resign thy breath ;
> Spirit, cast thy cares away ;
>   Dust, be thou dissolved in death.
> Thus the mighty Savior speaks
>   While the faithful Christian dies ;
> Thus the bonds of life he breaks,
>   And the ransomed captive flies."

Since the death of Mrs. Stewart at Cooperstown, the work of civilization and reformation in the Sandwich Islands has been rapidly progressing. The faith of the Church has been strong and confident, and she has exerted herself to save those islands from barbarism and ignorance. In her holy strength, and with her high commission, she has sent out her servants armed with the whole Christian armor. These men and women have preached Jesus and the cross with wonderful success. Struggling against the tide of obstacles and the barriers which sin raised in their pathway, they have advanced until they have caused an entire change in the customs and the religion of the people.

Nor have the natives been unwilling to render their assistance. They have coöperated with the missionaries, and nobly exerted themselves to bring the islands under Christian influences. Their efforts to erect temples in which they and their children may worship the only living and true God illustrate the zeal with which they toiled to accomplish good. Speaking of the large stone church at Honolulu, — a church which cost twenty thousand dollars, and required the labor of many men for six long years to finish it, — Mr. Bingham says, " In the erection of this stately edifice, the active men, among about one thousand communicants of that church, having divided into five companies, labored by rotation many days and weeks with patience and zeal."

Of the labor given to the erection of a house of worship at Kealakekua, the same work furnishes us with the following particulars : —

" The stones were carried upon the shoulders of men forty or fifty rods. The coral for making the lime they procured by diving in two or three fathom water and detaching blocks, or fragments. If these were too heavy for the diver to bring up to his canoe with his hands, he ascended to the surface to take breath, then descended with a rope, attached it to his prize, and, mounting to his canoe, heaved up the mass from the bottom, and, when the canoe was thus laden, rowed it ashore and discharged his freight. By this process they procured about thirty cubic fathoms, or seven thousand seven hundred and seventy-six cubic feet. To burn this mass, the church members brought from the mountain side, upon their shoulders, forty cords of wood. The lime being burned, the women took it in calabashes, or large gourd shells, and bore it on their shoulders to the place of building; also sand and water for making the mortar. Thus about seven hundred barrels each of lime, sand, and water, making about two thousand barrels, equal to three hundred and fifty wagon loads, were carried by women a quarter of a mile, to assist the men in building the temple of the Lord, which they desired to see erected for themselves and for their children — a heavy service, which they, their husbands, fathers, sons, had not the means of hiring nor teams to accomplish. The latter had other work far more laborious to perform for the house. The sills, posts, beams, rafters, &c., which they cut in the mountains, six to ten miles distant, they drew down by hand. The posts and beams required the strength of forty to sixty men each. Such a company, starting at break of day, with ropes in hand, and walking two or three hours through the fern and underbrush loaded with the cold dew, made fast to their timber, and, addressing themselves to their sober toil for the rest of the day, dragged it over beds of lava, rocks, ravines and rubbish, reaching the place of building about sunset."

Mr Coan gives the following amusing account of the industry and willingness of the people in church building at Waiakea, Hilo: "I have often gone with them to the forest, laid hold of the rope, and dragged timber with them from morning to night. On such occasions we usually, on our arrival at the timber to be drawn, unite in prayer, and then, fastening to the stick, proceed to work. Dragging timber in this way is exceedingly wearisome, especially if there be not, as is often the case, a full complement of hands. But what is wanting in numbers is often supplied in the tact and management of the natives, some of whom are expert in rallying, stimulating, and cheering their comrades, by sallies of wit, irony, and, if the expression is allowable, of good-natured sarcasm. The manner of drawing is quite orderly and systematic. They choose one of their number for a leader. This done, the leader proceeds to use his vocal powers by commanding all others to put theirs to rest. He then arranges his men on each side of the rope, like artillerists at the drag rope. Every man is commanded to grasp the rope firmly with both hands, straighten it, and squat down, inclined a little forward. The leader then passes from rear to front, and from front to rear, reviewing the line to see that every man grasps the rope. All is now still as the grave for a moment, when the commander, or marshal of the day, roars out in a stentorian voice, '*Kauo*, draw!' Every one then rises, and away dashes the timber, through thicket and mud, over lava and streamlet, under a burning sun or amidst drenching rain. No conversation is allowed except by the marshal, who seems to feel it his privilege, during his incumbency, to make noise enough for all."

In this toilsome way most if not all the houses for the public worship of God have been erected; and most of them being of enduring materials, they will stand for many years as monuments of the devotion, self-sacrificing industry, and sincere piety of the Sandwich Island Christians. A people having this spirit, and animated with such a love for Christ and his worship, could not fail in being successful while armed with gospel truth. Before such noble workmen all obstacles will vanish, all barriers will be broken down, all opposition will be overcome. Were the members of the church in Christian lands willing to make such sacrifices and perform such labors, a half century would not roll away ere the voice of the missionary would be heard in every valley and on every hill top of the globe. Were the Christians of one single denomination willing to lay hold upon the " drag rope " of Christian missions, and emulate the conduct of the poor, degraded Sandwich Islanders, in their efforts to build temples of worship, they would see the car of salvation moving on gloriously, and, ere long, would listen to the shout of a redeemed world.

The Christians of these islands seem to resemble the early disciples of our dear Savior. Their simple and unostentatious piety, their firm, manly devotion to truth, and steady resistance to error, their willingness to leave all for Christ, reminds us of the disciples of Antioch and Rome, who perilled life and happiness to prove their devotion to the cross. Perhaps nowhere in our times have converts from heathenism to Christianity displayed more of the primitive spirit, and developed more of the primitive virtues, than the once despised, idolatrous, blinded inhabitants of the Sandwich Islands. The language of each heart seems to be, —

> "Jesus, I my cross have taken,
> All to leave and follow thee;
> Naked, poor, despised, forsaken,
> Only thou my leader be."

In the language with which Mr. Bingham closes his full and valuable history, we close this sketch of the Sandwich Islands and of one of the most intelligent and gifted females ever sent to them: —

"A nation has been raised from blank heathenism to a rank among enlightened nations, to the enjoyment of letters and laws, of Christianity and the hope of heavenly glory. Whatever troubles may yet assail them, there is ground to rejoice that the foundation of the spiritual temple of Jehovah has there been firmly laid, and its superstructure commenced, which is to rise in future generations. The builders there and elsewhere have many adversaries; but the benignant Lamb shall overcome them. His servants must be multiplied, and many a heart, constrained by the love of Christ, will be found to say, —

'The voice of my departed Lord, "Go teach all nations,"
Comes on the night air, and awakes my ear.'

"If the American Board and its friends and laborers have not done too much for that nation in a generation past, — and who will say they have toiled or expended too much? — those who are on the Lord's side, grateful for what the Lord has *wrought* there, will be encouraged to attempt and expect the same or 'greater things than these' for other nations, till in every tongue they shall harmoniously hymn the Messiah's praise, and earth's ransomed millions shall swell the strain which these converted islanders have recently learned and gratefully adopted.

CHAPTER V.

SARAH L. SMITH,

OF SYRIA.

THERE are some spots on earth more hallowed than others. There are consecrated cities and towns, from which, as we approach them, we seem to hear a voice, saying, " Put off thy shoes; for the spot whereon thou treadest is holy ground."

Such are the places in which Christ our Savior lived, and preached, and suffered while incarnate. Such are the places where his immediate successors, the apostles and martyrs, contended so earnestly for the faith delivered to the saints. Jerusalem, Bethany, Bethlehem, Corinth, Ephesus, Antioch, and Rome will be associated forever, in the minds of Christians, with the early progress and triumphs of our holy religion; and the pious traveller will never visit those places without feeling his bosom thrill with tender and intense emotions.

On this account the mission in Syria is one of

peculiar interest. Founded almost within sight of Calvary, it is surrounded with many scenes of dear and hallowed interest; and it requires but little effort of the imagination to recall the song of the infant church, as it arose from vale and glen, vibrating on the air and echoing back from hoary Lebanon. It was with the mission in this place that the amiable, talented, and beloved subject of this article was connected.

Sarah Lanman Huntington was the daughter of Jabez Huntington, Esq. She was born in Norwich, Connecticut, on the 18th of June, 1802, and in that beautiful town passed through the period of childhood. She was educated with missionary sympathies and feelings. All the circumstances under which she was placed were calculated to invest the holy enterprise with sacred pleasantness. In her father's house she never heard a word of reproach breathed forth against the cause itself or the devoted men and women engaged in it. She traced her descent from the famous John Robinson, of Leyden, whose blood came flowing down through a long missionary line until it coursed in her veins. Her grandfather was a member of the American Board of Commissioners for Foreign Missions; and all her relatives on the side of father and mother were active promoters of the work of God.

Under such influences Sarah grew up, believing that it was far more honorable to do good to man, to be the means of reclaiming the wanderer from the path of duty, or to bring a sinner back to God, than to found an empire, or establish a throne, or conquer an army of steel-clad warriors, or lead in triumph captive kings and princes. Before her conversion, she was aware of the divine character of the work which had just commenced; and doubtless her young heart responded to the appeals made by the death of Harriet Newell and the life of Ann H. Judson.

During the first twelve years of her life there appears to be nothing unusual in her history. She was like other thoughtful and pleasant girls of her age, and spent her time in the amusements and pursuits of youth. At school she was industrious, studious, but not remarkably rapid in her progress; at home she was fondly loved and cherished; but in the minds of her parents she never appeared to be a *prodigy* or a *genius*.

At the age of twelve she became the subject of the Spirit's influence. Her mind was drawn to divine things and her heart touched by the finger of God. On the 10th of August, 1820, she realized for the first time the blessedness of full and free forgiveness. The Savior was precious to her soul, and holy duties were pleasant and delightful. She had passed from the deep waters of conviction, and gladly placed her feet on the Rock of Ages, where she stood immovable. Her joy knew no bounds.

Liberated from sin, free from the dreadful weight of guilt and condemnation, pardoned by God and loved by Christ, she deemed no praises too exalted, no trials too severe to endure in return. She immediately recognized the great principle that "we are not our own," and acted upon it; and life became from that hour devoted to holy employments and useful pursuits.

Writing to one of her friends about this time, she says, "All is changed. I am in a new world of thought and feeling. I begin to live anew. Even our beautiful Norwich has new charms, and, in sympathy with my joyousness, wears a new, a lovelier, aspect."

The vows which she made, as she passed through the "strait gate" and entered the kingdom of heaven, did not consist of words alone. They were engraven on her heart and carried out in her life as well as recorded on high. Ceaselessly she sought out ways in which she might do good to the bodies and the souls of her fellow-creatures; and what her hands found to do, she did with her might. In 1827 she formed a plan to benefit the Mohegan Indians, who lived a few miles from Norwich. These Indians were the remnant of a once mighty tribe; and the proud blood of some of their rude chieftains of former times coursed through the veins of these tattered and ragged descendants. From hut to hut she visited among these degraded children of the forest; started a Sabbath school, of which she and another young lady were the sole teachers; provided books for those who could read; and in many ways conferred benefits upon them. Not satisfied with this, she determined to build a church and secure the services of a missionary; and for this purpose wrote to several of her influential friends, to secure their coöperation and sympathy. For aid in her work of benevolence she also applied to the legislature of Connecticut and to the general government. To a considerable extent she was successful, and obtained the esteem and gratitude of that forlorn and oppressed people.

The manner in which she visited among the people gives us an insight into the character of the woman, and furnishes us with a clew to her future success. She usually rode from Norwich on horseback, and, taking a little girl with her into the saddle, passed from house to house, using the child as guide, interpreter, and adviser. When she met in the road a few ragged natives or a knot of men and women she would stop her horse and converse a while with them, and slip a tract into the hand of each, and with a smile pass on. In this way she gained the confidence and love of the poor people who lived in ignorance and degradation within sight of the towers and temples of New England towns and cities.

At times the mind of Miss H. was much exercised

in relation to a mission in the western part of our own country. The gathering thousands who were pouring in from every quarter of the world, the future influence of the west upon the nation, the wide field of usefulness there presented, were all inducements for her to go forth and labor amid the mountains and on the broad prairies which extend towards the shores of the Pacific Ocean.

The idea of laboring in the west was abandoned in 1833, during which year she resolved to accompany Rev. Eli Smith to his field of toil in Syria. The opportunity presented by the offer of Mr. Smith was what Miss H. most earnestly desired. Her heart was set on doing good; and no spot on earth could have been selected more in accordance with her tastes and feelings. The long-cherished purpose could now be accomplished; and, after due consultation with her friends, she was married on the 21st of July, in the midst of her associates, at Norwich.

On the 29th of August the parting between child and parents took place, and Mrs. Smith left the home of her infancy forever, and, after visiting the friends of her husband in Boston, embarked from that place for Malta, on the 21st of September, in the brig George, commanded by Captain Hallet.

The scene on board the vessel was peculiarly solemn. After the missionaries had arrived and the people had assembled on the deck and on the wharf all united in singing that grand hymn, —

> "Roll on, thou mighty ocean,
> And, as thy billows flow,
> Bear messengers of mercy
> To every land below."

Rev. Dr. Jenks then led in prayer, commending the servants of God to the gracious care of Him who sitteth on high; after which the brig was loosened from her moorings and floated down the harbor, while the little cluster of missionaries on board sung sweetly the beautiful hymn of Heber, —

> "From Greenland's icy mountains,
> From India's coral strand."

The sorrowful friends remained standing upon the wharf until the vessel which contained the loved ones had faded from sight, and with its precious freight was far out upon the deceptive ocean.

After a fine voyage of fifty-four days the missionaries landed at Malta, and proceeded to Beyroot, via Alexandria. They arrived at Beyroot on the 28th of January, 1834. The sketch of their voyage, given by Mrs. Smith herself and found in her published memoir, is of intense interest. The objects of interest were so numerous, the mind of the voyager so well prepared to appreciate them, that a journey on land could scarcely have been more delightful. The heaving Atlantic; the calm, bright Mediterranean; the Azore Islands; the long coast of Africa; the Straits of Gibraltar; the stay at Malta; the visits to convents, temples, and other places of resort; the city of Alexandria; the Mahometan Sabbath; the grave of Parsons; the passage to Beyroot, and the safe arrival, — were all calculated to enlist the feelings of such a woman, with such a mind, as Mrs. Smith. She arrived at her new residence at Beyroot on the 28th of January, 1834. The town lies at the foot of the "goodly mountain," Lebanon, and, to the approaching traveller, presents a scene of beauty seldom equalled. Descending gently from the south, the whole town seems like one vast garden, with houses half covered by the thick foliage, and cottages of Oriental style, of brown or yellow appearance, peeping through the overhanging trees, or standing in the centre of a well-cultivated spot, like a temple in the heart of a city. Away beyond is Lebanon, stretching its sunny ridges from north to south, and lifting its peaks until they bathe their foreheads in the clouds. On its sides are seen the cottage, and here and there a cluster of human habitations, forming little villages, which delight the eye and give beauty to the prospect. Every thing, to a native of Europe or America, is unique and strange.

and has an air of richness and productiveness which surprises while it charms. The birds, the beasts, the insects are, to a lover of natural beauty, sources of study and profit; and the refined mind could scarcely find a more delightful spot as a field of missionary exertion.

The inhabitants did not correspond with the outward scenery. Though the people kindly welcomed them, the missionaries found a wide difference in the habits and customs of the European and the Arab; and brought into connection with the latter, as they were every hour of the day, the contrast was continually before the mind.

Besides this, the missionary cannot live on the same equality with the people as can other classes of European or American residents. The *trader* can close his doors and have his family circles sacred from the intrusion of officious, meddlesome natives; but this course would defeat the very object which the *missionary* has in view. It would shut him out from the confidence and sympathy of those whose hearts he wished to reach. It would place between him and the heathen a barrier which would be insurmountable. So our sister found it at Beyroot. She had no house which she could properly call her own; for at times, while she was least prepared and while visits were least desirable, her house would be invaded by a company of five or six women, who would remain a long time, asking questions and prying into a hundred things which did not concern them.

And yet Mrs. Smith felt that these annoyances must be endured with cheerfulness; and when patience was almost wearied out, and time which belonged to herself and her family was taken up by such persons, she would console herself that such privations and trials were parts of the missionary work, which must be endured cheerfully for the sake of Jesus.

The manners, customs, and dresses of the people at Beyroot served to remind the Christian of the times of Christ, and led back the imagination through the lapse of eighteen hundred years to the thrilling events which transpired throughout the Holy Land.

So few are the improvements made in art and agriculture that one can easily fancy himself in the middle of the first century, gazing upon the people who from apostolic lips listened to the words of life and salvation; and under this almost irresistible impression the solemnity of Gethsemane and Calvary gathers over the soul, and throws a divine enchantment over the life and labors of the men of God. So our sister felt, as the Oriental costumes passed before her, as she looked out from her window upon the sides of the snow-covered Lebanon.

The situation of Mrs. Smith was not at all like

that of many other devoted servants of God. She was not compelled to break up the fallow ground, or be the first to drop the seed into the soil. Others had preceded her — they had prepared the way — they had erected the kindly shelter — they had opened the heathen mind to receive light and truth. Hence, on her arrival, she found all the comforts and conveniences of a civilized community — she found a most beautiful and romantic residence, a land teeming with all the hallowed associations of sacred history.

Called by God, not to the dungeons of Ava, not to the damp and monster-covered banks of the Irrawaddy, but to a more congenial field of labor, she toiled on in it with pleasure.

Mrs. Smith spent most of the time in her school, which was commenced soon after her arrival, and for a while was "the only schoolmistress in all Syria." The school house, which was erected upon a plan of her own, was filled by a large number of children of Egyptian, Arabian, and Turkish parents, who, under the care of their faithful teacher, made considerable progress. To instruct the little, ignorant children, explain to them the mysteries of science, and lead them upward to the God who made them, was a task for which she was well adapted. Being an ardent lover of the beautiful and grand in nature, she made the green fields, the blooming vineyards, the high, towering mountain all subservient to the purposes of instruction. Her residence among the Mohegans prepared her for her duties in Syria, and gave her the advantage of an experience which she could have acquired nowhere else. In the Sabbath school she was also most happily employed in instructing the fifteen or twenty children who attended in the path of holiness. Under her labors the school gradually and constantly increased, and a visible change for good was observed among the pupils. Her kindness and affection won the hearts even of the Moslem parents, who, in repeated instances, disobeyed the direction of their priests, and kept their children under her care after the school had been condemned.

One of the most pleasant circumstances connected with the missionary life of Mrs. Smith was her visit to the Holy Land in 1835. From early childhood she had regarded with a feeling of veneration the city of Jerusalem. That was the city in which many of the Savior's miracles were done; there he had healed the sick, cast out devils, raised the dead, and performed many other wonderful works; there was the temple; there the scene of trial, and the streets along which the cross was borne; there, near at hand, was the Garden of Gethsemane, the Mount of Olives, and on the other side of the city the Hill of Calvary on which the Savior was crucified. When, therefore, she found herself on her journey to the most noted spot in the wide world emotions of solemn and pleasing interest crowded upon her mind. As she passed along, one object of interest after another presented itself. Tyre and Sidon were seen; and the spot whereon Sarepta once stood was crossed. Her feet traversed the mountains of Galilee, and stood upon the summit of Carmel, Gerizim, Tabor, Hermon, Lebanon, Olivet, and Calvary. She visited the spots where tradition tells us the Savior perished and where his sufferings were endured; and doubtless her imagination brought back the scenes of the past, and she might have heard the low, silvery tones of mercy and grace as they flowed from the lips of "Him who spake as never man spake."

After visiting the prominent places of the Holy Land, our missionary returned again to her station at Beyroot, where she labored with untiring diligence until June, 1836, when, her health failing, she set sail with her husband for Smyrna, with the delusive hope of regaining it. At this point her sufferings commenced. The vessel in which they sailed was old and uncomfortable; the crew and some of the passengers were any thing but agreeable; and horrid profanity was heard instead of prayer and praise. The fifth night after leaving Beyroot the vessel was wrecked on the north side of the Island of Cyprus, and the voyagers escaped with their lives. After many hardships and much danger they landed on a sandy shore in an almost destitute condition, and, after continuing on the island some days, obtained passage towards the place of their destination. The vessel on board which they sailed was a Turkish lumberman, and in no way adapted to the conveyance of passengers. But, submitting to stern necessity, they made the best improvement of the circumstances under which they were placed. Of the voyage Mr. Smith says, " The wind was high, and, being contrary to the current, raised a cross and troublous sea. The vessel was terribly tossed, and, being slightly put together, threatened to founder at almost every plunge. Mrs. Smith, besides rolling to and fro for want of something to support her against the motion, was writhing under violent seasickness, which, instead of allaying, served only to increase her cough. She had some fears that she should not survive the night; and for a time I did not know what would be the end of her sufferings."

They arrived at Smyrna in thirty-three days after they left Beyroot. Here her strength gradually failed. The consumption which was wasting her body and drawing her down to the grave made visible advances; and on the 30th of September, 1836, she died in the triumphs of faith, at Boojah, a quiet little village about five miles from Smyrna.

In her sickness she gave the most cheering

illustrations of the power of the Christian faith to subdue fear and disarm death. Her mind was lifted up above the sufferings of her lot, and she held constant intercourse with the Savior of her soul. To a great extent she was free from pain, and enabled to converse with her husband upon the prospect before her. She waited for death with pleasure, and was ready at any hour to depart and be with Jesus. To die was gain, unspeakable gain; and she knew it well. Hence, when her physician and friends would whisper words of hope, she would plainly tell them that her work was done, her mission fulfilled, and the sand of her glass almost run out. It gave her more pleasure to look forward to a meeting with the loved men and women who had departed than to contemplate an existence on the earth, where storms will disturb the fairest prospect, and clouds will shut out the rays of the noonday sun.

On the Sabbath before her death she sung, in company with her husband, the hymn, —

> "Thine earthly Sabbaths, Lord, we love;
> But there's a nobler rest above;
> To that our longing souls aspire
> With cheerful hope and strong desire."

At twenty minutes before eight o'clock she died, with a countenance all illuminated with smiles, which, after she ceased to speak, played upon her features, and by their silent eloquence whispered to every beholder, "Though I walk through the valley of the shadow of death, I will fear no evil."

On the following day, as the tidings spread through Smyrna that the sainted woman was at rest, the flags of the American vessels in the harbor were seen lowering to half mast, and that upon the dwelling of the consul was shrouded with the drapery of death.

On the 1st of October she was carried to the grave. The service of the English church was read beside the corpse, and in one common grief the people stood bending over it, while the beautiful hymn of Dr. Watts was sung — "Unveil thy bosom, faithful tomb."

The tidings came echoing across the deep, and in our homes the story of death was told; and sadness filled the pious heart as the thought that another servant of God, another heroine of the church, had fallen at her post, a martyr in the cause of truth. The American Board of Commissioners for Foreign Missions felt deeply the loss which had been sustained, and mourned for one whose piety, intellect, and labors were abundant.

Here end the missionary toils of two years and four months: and, uttering words of peace to the fallen, we bid farewell to her memory until death shall call us to join the blessed throng of the ransomed whose names are recorded on high.

CHAPTER VI.

ELEANOR MACOMBER,

OF BURMAH.

ALMOST all the heroines who have gone forth from the churches of America to dot heathen soil with their lowly graves have been attended by some stronger arm than that of weak, defenceless woman. Many of them have had husbands on whom they relied for support and protection, and to whom they could turn with the assurance of sympathy in hours of anguish and gloom.

But Miss Macomber went out attended by no such kind companion. She resolved on a missionary life, without the offer of marriage being connected with it. No husband helped her decide the momentous question; and when she resolved, it was to go *alone*. Impelled by the Christian's high and holy motives, she determined on a course which would involve her in a thousand perplexities and load her with a thousand cares. With none to share these cares and perplexities, with no heart to keep time with the wild beatings of her own, she crossed, a friendless woman, the deep, dark ocean, and on soil never trodden by the feet of Christian men erected the banner of the cross.

Eleanor Macomber was born at Lake Pleasant, Hamilton county, New York. Here her childhood and youth were passed, and here was her mind prepared for that career of usefulness which in after years made her an ornament to her sex, to the church, and to the world.

From Lake Pleasant she removed to Albany, where her heart was brought into subjection to the divine will and her mind impressed with the great truths of revelation. She became a convert to the religion of the cross. She became a convert to tears, to prayers, to self-denying labors, to a life of sacrifice and devotion. Her piety was from henceforth of the highest character, and all her daily deportment gave evidence of her love to the Savior.

In 1830 she was sent out by the Missionary Board, of the Baptist denomination, as a teacher among the Ojibwas, at Sault de Ste. Marie, in Michigan. This was her first missionary work, and she continued engaged in it nearly four years, when, in the mysterious providence of God, her health failed, and she was obliged to return to her friends. But the great Head of the church, in removing her from one field of labor, was only preparing her for another. In 1836 she became connected with the Karen mission, and a more extended field of usefulness was thrown open before her. She sailed from this country in the ship Louvre, and arrived in Maulmain in the autumn of the same year.

After her arrival she was stationed at Dong-Yahn, about thirty-five miles from Maulmain. Here she lived and labored almost alone, doing the great work which was assigned her. In the midst of discouragements she fainted not, but performed labors and endured afflictions almost incredible. When she arrived at the scene of her future labors her heart was affected at what she saw. Vice and sin reigned triumphant. The most odious, disgusting, and blasphemous crimes were committed. On every hand intemperance and sensuality were observable. She immediately commenced in their midst the worship of God. On the Sabbath the people were drawn together to hear about the blessed Jesus; and the story of the cross was told with all the sweetness of woman's piety. During the week her house was thrown open for morning and evening prayers. A school was soon gathered under her persevering labors: ten or twelve pupils gathered into it.

Mr. Osgood, who accompanied Miss Macomber from Maulmain to her field of labor, and whose duty required him to leave her there, an unprotected stranger, in the midst of a brutal, drunken community of heathen barbarians, writes as follows of her place of toil and her feelings on her arrival: —

"We ascended the Salwen River about twenty-five miles, and slept in our boats the first night. On the morning of the next day, December 20, we procured a guide and proceeded overland, following the line of the Zuagaben Mountains, to the house of one of the chiefs, about ten miles. The chief and most of the inhabitants were absent, attending the burning of a Burman priest. I immediately despatched a messenger for him, and in the mean time took up lodgings in his house, to wait his return. Two or three men and several females and children spent the greater part of the afternoon and evening with us, hearing sister M. read from the books which have already been written in their language. We, however, soon found that we had arrived in a most unpropitious time; for almost every man in the vicinity was in a state of beastly intoxication.

"On the morning of the 21st, as the chief did not arrive, we concluded to return about half way to the river, with a view to exploring the country, and in hopes of meeting the chief on his return, and holding a conference with him and several other principal men relative to the objects of the mission. Having proceeded as far as we intended, and waited some time in vain for his arrival, I concluded to go in person and endeavor to prevail upon him to return, as my business would not allow of protracted absence from home. On arriving at the place of the feast we found a large concourse of people, consisting of Burmans, Peguans, Karens, and Toung-thoos, who were assembled upon an extensive plain to pay the last tribute of respect to a Burman priest that had been some months dead and was now to be burned. The body was mounted upon an immensely large car, decorated according to Burman custom, to which were attached ropes made of grass, three or four hundred feet long. With these the car was drawn about the plain, levelling, in its course, every obstacle.

"After some little search we found the chief men, the objects of our pursuit, but so completely drunk that all attempts to induce them to return with us were entirely fruitless. We immediately returned to the house of the chief where we had lodged the previous night. In the evening the chief returned, but so intoxicated as to be entirely unfit for business.

"We rose early on the morning of the 22d to take advantage of the effect of the night's rest upon our host, and obtained the privilege of a few minutes' conversation. He gave us permission to build in any place we saw fit to select; but before I had fixed upon a place he was again missing. After selecting a place and making the necessary preparations for building, I prepared to return to Maulmain. Until this time our dear sister Macomber had borne the trials of the journey and the prospect of being left alone without the least appearance of shrinking; but when the moment of separation came, the thought of being left, without a friend, in the midst of a drunken people, and even in the house of a man completely besotted with ardent spirits, and at a distance of thirty miles or more from any civilized society, with scarcely a sufficient knowledge of the language to make known her wants, was too much for the delicate feelings of a female to endure; and she could only give vent to the emotions of her heart by a flood of tears. She soon, however, recovered her self-possession, and resolved to cast herself upon the merciful protection of her heavenly Father, and to pursue what seemed to her to be the path of duty."

But the laborer did not long toil in vain. In less than one year, a church of natives, converted through her instrumentality, was formed and placed under the care of Rev. Mr. Stephens. The people changed beneath the influence of divine grace. Intemperance, sensuality, and other vices gradually disappeared; and morality, solemnity virtue, and religion took their places. The Sabbath day was respected; and in the jungle and thicket the voice of prayer was often heard. Jesus and the cross received thought; and the great idea of salvation by grace was pondered and believed.

In a few months the little church planted through her instrumentality numbered more than twenty persons, who continued faithful in the duties and practices of the disciples. Her feelings towards the little band of Christians gathered by her in the very wilderness of sin are represented as having been very strong and earnest. Her language was, when speaking of the church, —

> "For her my tears shall fall,
> For her my prayers ascend,
> To her my toils and cares be given,
> Till toils and cares shall end."

She was an *intelligent* missionary. Her mind was of superior order, and reason held even balance. Her zeal for the truth was not a blind, headlong enthusiasm, which sparkles, and glistens, and comes to an end, but a zeal founded on the wants and woes of a perishing world. She measured the depths of heathen degradation and estimated the worth of souls, and went to work calmly, philosophically, and earnestly.

The faith which she carried forth was well studied and fully understood. She had a reason to give for the hope which was in her and which she so fondly cherished. She was able to defend it — to develop its glories — to show its superiority to any and all the forms of heathenism. The kindness of her own heart led her not only to appreciate the superior excellence of the gospel, but also to feel most deeply for the degraded Karens. Towering far above them in the majesty of intellect and the grandeur of thought, she sought to inspire them with feelings kindred to her own. Her high ambition was, to lift the race from its fallen position, save the people from their prevalent vices, enlighten the minds of the young, and improve and regenerate the hearts of all.

She thought it not inconsistent with her true dignity, as a woman possessing a high order of intellect, to bring her mind into contact with the most degraded of the human family, if by so doing she could be the means of saving some and improving others. Hence she *studied* to do good. The energies of her mind were placed under contribution to furnish arguments by which the heathen mind might be convinced and the heathen heart subdued. She met the strongest objections to the new faith; she answered the questions of the cavilling priest; she reasoned with the common people from the law and the gospel, until enough were converted to form a church of our Lord Jesus.

She was a *laborious* missionary. Al. our missionaries are laborers. The work itself compels toil; and it cannot be avoided. But few go into it with an idea of ease and personal aggrandizement; and that few are disappointed. The great enterprise is in itself a hardship; and however cheerfully it may be borne for Jesus and a dying world, it cannot be carried on without immense labor and sacrifice on the part of the missionaries.

But the noble woman of whom we write was in labors more abundant. She even went beyond what was expected of a most faithful servant of God: she exerted herself to an extent which but few others have done, and gathered a reward in proportion to her labors. Others have suffered more and had a more checkered life; but none have put forth greater exertions to accomplish a given result.

Indeed, the spectacle of a weak, friendless, lone woman removing from Maulmain to Dong-Yahn, and there, with no husband, no father, no brother, establishing public worship, opening her house for prayer and praise, and gathering schools in the midst of wild and unlettered natives, is one full of moral grandeur. The idea of performing such a work alone, the idea of a defenceless woman going into a besotted nation, among a drunken, sensual people, and lifting them up to the privileges of a refined faith, a pure religion, is an idea worthy of an angel. This idea entered the mind of our subject, became a part of herself, and was carried out in her life.

Not content with sitting down and teaching all

who came to her, she went out to the surrounding tribes, and, for miles around, preached salvation to the dying. In these excursions she was generally attended by one or two converts, who formed her escort and guard, and performed that part of the labor which could not be brought within the province of woman. In this heroic and romantic manner she travelled from place to place, fording rivers, crossing deep ravines, climbing high hills and mountains, entering the dwellings of the poor, sitting beside the bed of the dying, rebuking the sinful, and every where preaching the doctrines of salvation.

The spectacle was one which affected even the heathen heart; and this estimable woman was respected and loved even by those who scorned the gospel and hated Christ. She had "a more excellent way;" and that excellence was exhibited in every step of her progress. As she approached the towns and villages, on her excursions of mercy, she was often met by enthusiastic crowds, who welcomed her with joy, and led her to the homes of the dying, and besought her aid. Most females would have fainted under her toils and turned back from the amount of work to be performed; but gifted with wisdom and strength from on high, endowed with powers not her own, she continued until a church was gathered and the foundation laid for a prosperous mission.

She was a *pious* missionary. Doubtless much of the success which crowned the efforts of Miss Macomber must be attributed, not to the brilliancy of her intellect, not to the vigor of her mind, not to the vast labor performed, but to the *piety* of her heart. It was this which induced her to go out; she had no other motive in leaving home and all the joys of kindred and native land. It was this that induced her to plant the cross where the name of Jesus had not been preached; to go alone, a friendless woman, in the midst of savages; to brave sickness, disease, and death itself, in order to utter notes of salvation which should fall on dying ears like strains from heaven. It was this which sent her, like an angel of mercy, to the homes of the weary, to the abodes of sickness, to the hovels of want, to dens of crime, to whisper rebuke in one place and consolation in another.

She gave ample evidence that her heart had been baptized in the Holy Spirit; that her mind had come into contact with the great truths of revelation; that she had been to the cross and received an impulse from the spectacle of death there witnessed; that her heart had bled at scenes of woe which every where abound on heathen soil; that, in the majesty of humble faith and trust in the Divinity, she had resolved to die in the holy work to which God and the church had assigned her.

We not unfrequently behold the most lovely

exhibitions of piety in Christian communities. We see religion doing its holy work in the lives of its professors; we contemplate instances of piety and devotion which seem to be more of heaven than earth; but never can be witnessed in Christian lands those sublime trophies of godliness which we find on shores which are covered with heathen abomination. We must leave home, we must cross the ocean, we must follow Harriet Newell through all her sufferings, until she finds an early grave. We must follow Ann H. Judson to the dungeons of Ava, to the damp, cold prisons of the East, to her home of suffering and death. We must trace the course of Miss Macomber from Maulmain to her new residence at Dong-Yahn; we must see her on her excursions into the surrounding province, and listen to her teachings as around her a rude group gather to hear of Jesus.

Here is piety in its most lovely form. Here is godliness in its most divine attire. Here is pure religion, which is undefiled before God. In these cases we see what cannot be witnessed at home, and what thousands of pious women would shrink from as impracticable and impossible.

Amid such scenes as these Miss Macomber seems to rise above the measure of a human being, and gain a likeness to Him who went about doing good. She appears superior to the infirmities of humanity, because she was engaged in an employment so nearly resembling that of her divine Master, and performed it with so much of the excellence and beauty of his spirit and grace.

Perhaps no better description of Miss Macomber as a laborer in the vineyard of her Lord can be given than she herself furnishes in her printed letters, which are found scattered through the missionary magazines of the denomination to which she belonged.

"DONG-YAHN, April 15, 1837.

" A line to you the last of December left me at this place, in the house of a Karen chief, waiting the building of my own, and giving what little religious instruction my knowledge of the language would admit. I have now the happiness to inform you that the excitement, which I then attributed wholly to novelty, proved to be a gracious influence of the Holy Spirit. A number of these poor, dark heathen, who were then bound in Satan's double chain, (idolatry and drunkenness,) have been liberated and brought into the glorious liberty of the gospel of Christ, and are now rejoicing in hope of the glory of God. Ten have been baptized, four men and six women; and a number of others, I trust, will ere long seek the blessed privilege. Many are still inquiring, and some, I trust, earnestly seeking. But many are opposing, reviling, and persecuting; and a few are indifferent and unconcerned.

"The progress of the work has been deeply interesting to all who have been acquainted with it, and particularly so to myself. Never were the power and mercy of God more manifestly displayed, and never did his saving grace shine through a more feeble instrumentality. But God can work according to his will; and, blessed be his name, the heathen shall be given to his Son.

"Our first baptism was on the 12th of January. Chung-pau, a man rather advanced in years, but of a sound, good mind, and who has thus far manifested a most devoted spirit, had from the first listened with uncommon interest; and I think I shall never forget the sensations it gave me when he would come and sit down by me, and, with a countenance which bespoke a soul awakened to the interest of eternal realities, would ask, 'What is it to believe? What can *I* do to believe? I want to escape hell and obtain heaven. I wish to trust in Jesus Christ. What shall I do?' O, what would I have given in that moment for an easy use of the language! But I said what I could; and the Spirit taught him as man could not.

"On the 21st of January brother Osgood came up again, and had the happiness to baptize six more; viz., Ah-wah and wife, Bah-mee and wife, and Ko-pee and wife; and Mr. Judson baptized three of the chief's daughters on the 16th of March, one only about twelve years old. All gave good evidence of a gracious change, and have since manifested a growing devotion to the cause. A number of others of the chief's children, I trust, have been made partakers of divine grace, and will ere long enter the visible church. One of those baptized was married; and although her husband made no objections to her baptism, yet he immediately left her. She has two young children, whom her father has added to his eleven; and it is truly interesting to see the care he personally takes of them. Bahmee has also been turned off by his widowed mother without a spoonful of rice for his family, (wife and two children;) and yet I hear not a hard or murmuring word. They seem to take it as a thing of course, that, if they *will* be disciples, they must suffer persecution.

"When I consider these and many other things which these dear Christians meet with, I cannot but admire the power of divine grace, and find new cause to bless God for light and civilization.

"The men baptized all expressed a great desire to devote their future lives to the service of God in making known his great salvation to those who were ignorant of it. They have uniformly manifested the same spirit ever since, and have been very useful so far as they knew. I have spared no pains in giving them every opportunity in my power for religious instruction; and their progress has been truly pleasing. The chief and Bah-mee both read Peguan well, and Burman some; and have now learned to read and write their own language. The former is about forty, of respectable talents and considerable influence. Bah-mee, who I think is an uncommonly able man, is about thirty; was in the priest's office three years, but left them some years ago; and when I came here was fast pursuing the drunkard's road with all the others. Ko-pee is but little over twenty, but has a wife and two children. He knows nothing of letters, but possesses a quick, discerning mind, and a lovely disposition. He is learning to read; and I am making great efforts to have the old man (Chung-pan) learn to read. I hope to get them all to Maulmain during the rains, that they may have better advantages for religious instruction, and that those who can may get a good knowledge of Burman books. They all understand considerable of the language; and it will be long before there will be books to any extent in their own. It has all the time seemed to me an indication of designs of great mercy towards this people that men of such qualifications should be called just at the commencement of labors amongst them; and I trust that God will so direct that they may accomplish much for the salvation of their countrymen and the glory of his name.

"I have had two or three Burman assistants constantly, who not only go out in the vicinity, accompanied by some of the Karens, and preach daily, but make excursions of four or five days in the villages, amongst the mountains, preaching the gospel to Toung-thoos, Peguans, or Burmans, as they happen to meet with them. I have made it my personal business to go with some of them; so that I have visited all the families within six or seven miles once or twice. I trust that these labors, though feeble, have not been in vain. I can speak but little of the language; but keeping a Karen with me, who is accustomed to my broken speeches, I give him ideas which he explains; and have been comforted and happy in the work, though attended with much fatigue and exposure.

"These things have not gone forward without opposition, as you will readily suppose. Besides all that would be expected from a numerous and deeply interested priesthood, we have had the fierce and violent opposition of a young prophet, who started up just before my arrival, and is located about a mile from me. He renounces a little of Boodhism and adds some other things; is unlettered and of no marked character; and yet he has many very devoted adherents. It is believed, however, by the best judges that he will be of short continuance. He effectually evades every effort to make him hear the gospel. His followers do not permit us to ascend the ladder into his house; and I have been out sometimes two or three days in succession, and have not been permitted to enter more than ten or twelve houses. It was fatiguing and painful to be exposed to the sun or hot air so long, and to find a seat as I could on the ground; but I was never comfortless or unhappy, assured that I was going at the bidding of Him who exposed his life unto death for a guilty world.

"We have had morning and evening worship from the first, and four or five exercises on the Sabbath, usually in Peguan, interpreted into Karen. I often ask questions at the close. A school has been sustained by my teacher, who, though very incompetent, has done very well. We have about a dozen scholars, as none will come who are opposed to us."

The following letter was written at Dong-Yahn February 5, 1838, and published shortly afterwards in this country : —

"The work of God is still going on here. Three men requested baptism last Sabbath, and a number more will soon come forward. This is the more encouraging, as, just now, there is an unusual effort of the adversary to put the cause down. It is the season for funeral festivals; and for fifteen or twenty days they have been in constant celebration, which of course attracts much attention. But the priests, not finding their coffers so well filled as usual, have seemed to make an effort as for life; and there is no end to the fog of worthless stuff which comes from them. It would seem that there was very little else said or done than what their violence called forth. No one of the Christians can go abroad but they hear from every quarter '*Jesus Christ*,' by way of contempt; and all who attend our meetings receive the same treatment unless they join the rabble. So that when any of them decide to come out and face the whole, which to a heathen is mountainous, there is strong evidence that divine grace has taken possession of their hearts.

"One woman had made up her mind to come forward, but said she feared she could not endure to be cast off, not only by her parents and relatives, but by the whole village, as they had told her they would do. So she concluded to wait and see how her mind was when the others were baptized.

"Have been absent considerably of late, wishing to visit all the villages just about the mountain. Found ten or twelve places of some importance: this, however, is the largest and most important, except Tun-pah-tine, where we have one convert, and where I spent four days last week. There are some encouraging indications there; but the chiefs will not yet consent to my building a zayat. I am trying to get some of the converts to go and build there; but they are so timid and deficient in energy that, if left to themselves, I do not know that they would ever go out of their own village though they never hesitate to go wherever I direct them. But in this case I wish them to take some responsibility.

"We have now an applicant for baptism from Pub-ong, a young man who has some excellent qualifications for usefulness. There are also two or three encouraging cases in Tun-loh, five or six miles distant, as also in some other directions; but the future is unknown.

"Our meeting is beginning to attract more attention, so that our room is often crowded; consequently I have engaged the chief to put on an addition of a few feet, which will be done this week.

"All the Christians seem to be getting on well. Bah-mee is my principal preacher. He certainly does admirably, considering what he was a year ago; but I find it necessary to see him, look over every subject, and give him all the ideas I wish to have advanced.

"There are constant rumors of robberies on the river, which of course prevent our doing any thing here."

Under date of July 30, 1838, we find the following article: —

"I still find much comfort and encouragement in trying to lead Karens in the path of knowledge and salvation. At the same time, I have constant cause to mourn over their defects and errors, which require not a little watchfulness and anxiety; but even in this I find a pleasure, having the assurance that I am not *alone.*

"In regard to the state of things at Dong-Yahn, Ko My-at-yaw, whom I left in charge, informs me that about all remain as when I left. The three or four who were rather hopeful still seem to be inquiring; opposition is about the same. There has been another attempt to burn the house, but unsuccessful. I have very little expectation that it will stand till my return; but this is but a secondary cause of anxiety. Their seeming determination to go down to eternal death causes me, at times, exquisite pain. O, when will they turn and live?

"The native Christians have generally, from the first, appeared remarkably firm and steadfast; and although some cases have required discipline, yet not one has had the appearance of contemplated or wilful sin. One poor old man alone, twelve or fifteen miles off, was overcome, by the long solicitation of a numerous family and under peculiar circumstances, so as to eat in a feast made to appease evil spirits; but he immediately came down here, confessed, and appeared truly humbled; said he did not forget God any moment, or cease to love him; but to be at peace with friends, he ate. I directed him to return and prove his sincerity by a future upright walk, and when we all returned, at the close of the rains, we would consult together on his case. There have been some other similar cases in regard to drinking — an evil which I fear more than all others.

"Agreeably to our earnest prayer, there seems to be an opening amongst the Pgwos at Bassein. I have prepared an assistant (Telaw) and family to go over to Rangoon two or three times; but they have been providentially prevented. We now wait with anxiety to hear from that quarter in regard to political affairs."

In November of the same year she writes as follows: "I may have mentioned that there had been attempts to burn the house and zayat at Dong-Yahn when we were in it. Since the rains ceased the attempt has been again repeated and considerable damage done; but I understand the chief thinks he can repair it for the dry season with but little expense; and I expect to build before another season, as the house was of the kind which usually lasts but two years. I thought it probable that the first attempt was in consequence of the increase of our number — brother and sister Brayton being then there; but now believe it was owing to a settled enmity to the gospel of Christ.

' Should not the power of God be displayed in changing the hearts of the perpetrators, or they be found out, I expect to be annoyed all the coming season, and have but little hope of keeping a house standing. Still the cause is God's; the hearts of men are in his hands. He can subdue them; and I believe he will, and that the gospel will yet triumph at Dong-Yahn. It has already done wonders; and the time cannot be far distant when the enemy will be put to silence. Two or three of the assistants have just returned from there, and give the most cheering accounts of the attention of numbers to the word. They say that the three or four inquirers appear well, and talk of being baptized. The chief, who remains there constantly, is very much encouraged, and appears truly devoted to the cause of Christ. Ko My-at-yau is also there; rather old and feeble, but a faithful laborer.

"I am not a little comforted in seeing the zeal and increased efficiency with which the natives go to their work since leaving school, (about six weeks ago.) Ko Chung-paw, Telaw, and Bah-mee have been out in different directions, and bring pleasing accounts. They spent three weeks in one town on a branch of the Dah Gyieng. They say they every where met with Karens; but they are very much scattered and very poor, having lately emigrated from the Shyán country, three or four days over the mountains. The Karens, to an individual, listened well, though Boodhists; and many expressed a desire to receive further instruction, so as to become Christians. An aged priest, highly esteemed among them, and who does not conform to all the customs of the Burman priests, would not release them short of two days, so anxious was he to hear. They left the Testament and other Burman books, and Ko Chung-paw gave him his eyeglasses. The old priest sent me presents and a request to visit them. I attempted to visit that region last season; but reports of robberies on the rivers prevented. It is not more than four or five tides from here. The assistants have just been sent to make them another visit, and to tell them that, if they wish for instruction, they must build a zayat."

At the close of the same year our laborious missionary gives to her supporters and patrons the following summary view of the Dong-Yahn station, with which she was connected, and in the prosperity of which she was so much interested: —

" I shall ever rejoice in what I have witnessed of the power of divine grace amongst the heathen. A number of precious souls have been rescued from Satan's power; and one, I trust, has gone home to heaven, though not permitted to join the church below.

" The native Christians here now number twenty

three, twelve of whom have been baptized the present year. A few are still inquiring; but the multitude are going on the broad way to eternal death.

"During the dry season the assistants visited, more than once, all the villages about these mountains; and I think, from what I could judge by spending most of the time with them, the truth was faithfully declared and the way of life made plain. At Tunpuhtine and Puhaung some have been gathered in; at Tunlopun are some hopeful cases, as well as at Pahleen and Pompeah.

"Evening and morning worship has been kept up all the time, and worship on the Sabbath, with Sabbath schools, &c.

"Bah-mee, whom I selected for the purpose from amongst the first converts, and who has thus far justified my expectations, has been my principal means of communication with the people. I have taken unwearied pains with him, giving him every means in my power for instruction; and I am daily comforted in seeing that it has not been in vain. He is much engaged about the vicinity we lately visited, on a branch of the Dah Gyieng, and I trust his labors there have been blessed. But experience has often shown that natives, however efficient with teachers, are but children if left alone.

"Ko Chung-paw, two years ago, was fast going down the declivity of life in all the darkness of heathenism; but a ray of heavenly light darted across his path, arrested his attention, and soon kindled to a flame. Now, I may say, he is a 'burning and a shining light;' one to whom we often point as a witness of the power and purity of the religion of Jesus Christ."

Miss Macomber died in April, 1840. The closing scenes of her life were full of sadness and full of glory. Her death was deeply lamented by those who knew her worth; and many of the Dong-Yahn women came to her funeral, crying, "The mamma is dead! the mamma is dead!" and with wails of sorrow surrounded her grave. They had listened to her counsels, they had experienced her kindness, they had partaken of her hospitality; and, though many of them did not love the Savior, they mourned the fall of his servant. Their nation had sustained an irreparable loss; and they came to pay their last tribute of respect to the ashes of the departed. The last hours of Miss Macomber are thus described by Rev. S. M. Osgood, who was at Maulmain at the time of her death. The account, from the pen of one who witnessed the whole scene, will be read with deep interest. Mr. Osgood says, —

"It becomes my painful duty to announce to you the death of our dear sister E. Macomber, who died with jungle fever on the evening of the 16th instant, after an illness of nine days aged thirty nine years.

"On the 9th of March Miss Macomber came down from Dong-Yahn with brother Stevens, and on the morning of the 10th left us again, with a view to visit a body of Pgwo Karens, residing high up one of the rivers. She had also a particular reference to spending the hottest part of the season *on* the river, having suffered much from the extreme heat at Dong-Yahn during the hot season last year. On the 4th instant she returned from this excursion, having enjoyed excellent health and a peculiarly pleasant season in labor for the good of the souls of the Karens, many of whom listened with much interest, and were 'almost persuaded to be Christians.'

"She arrived here late in the evening, and appeared quite well, with the exception of a slight cold, which she said she had taken that evening. On Sunday, the 5th, she complained of headache, but not so severe as to prevent her attendance upon the usual religious exercises of the day; and on Monday, after spending some hours with me in the bazaar, she left, and started on her return to Dong-Yahn. Before she arrived, however, her illness grew more violent, and, though it subsequently abated for a time, became again so decided that on the following Wednesday she was removed to this place by Christian Karens for the purpose of obtaining medical aid. Nothing remarkable or alarming was then discovered in her symptoms; and Doctor Charlton, the medical gentleman who was called in, expressed the fullest confidence that her disease would yield to the ordinary course of treatment, and that she would soon be able to resume her labors. But she thought otherwise; and although she did not express any conviction during two or three of the first days that the disease would prove fatal, she afterwards told me repeatedly that she had not from the first had the least expectation of recovery.

"On Saturday, the 11th instant, she, with the greatest composure, attended to the settlement of her temporal affairs, and then seemed to feel that her work was done. Her mind was perfectly clear and calm to the last; and during her whole illness she was a lovely example of Christian fortitude, patience, and resignation. Her faith was unwavering; and consequently she was enabled to look forward to the period of her dissolution with evident pleasure, and with the fullest conviction that death was but the door to endless bliss. I asked her if she felt any reluctance to die; and she replied, 'I have not the least. It is a pleasure to think of dying. I shall see much of what I have recently thought a little of — the glory of God and the love of Christ. When I think of the dear Karen disciples I feel for them, and would be willing to stay

with them a little longer; but if it is the Lord's
will that I should leave them, I have nothing to say.
Tell my friends I am not sorry that I came to this
country or that I came alone. I have suffered for
nothing which they could have supplied me with.
I have found kind friends to take care of me.' She
appeared upon the whole rather anxious to die, and
to die soon. The morning before her death, although
none of us thought she was so near her end, she
was heard to pray, 'O my Master, take me to
thyself this day.' While in the agony of death she
said, 'Why cannot I be released?' But when one
remarked, 'The Lord's time is the best time,' she
replied, 'Yes;' and after a few minutes more she
quietly fell asleep in Jesus.

"The dear Karen Christian disciples have suffered a great loss, which they most deeply feel.
Brother Stevens and I visited them a few days subsequent to her death and found them overwhelmed
with grief, but at the same time resolved to trust in
the Lord and go forward. They are a lovely band,
and apparently as well grounded in the principles
of religion as could be expected of any so recently
converted from heathenism."

Thus parted with earth one of the most devoted
servants of God. She has gone up on high to receive her reward. By her death the heathen lost a
most faithful friend, the Missionary Union lost a

most devoted laborer, and the cause of Christ parted with a most zealous advocate.

And shall we weep? No; death has gained no victory. God and the Christian have triumphed over death and the grave.

> "Well we know her living faith
> Had the power to conquer death;
> As a living rose may bloom
> By the borders of the tomb."

Her life was short, and her sun went down while it was yet day. But short as her stay on earth was, she was enabled to do much good; and in eternity many will rise up to call her blessed.

CHAPTER VII.

SARAH D. COMSTOCK,

OF BURMAH.

THE Burman empire has witnessed the death scene of some of the most illustrious women who have ever lived. It is the graveyard in which their bodies have been laid to rest after the spirits have departed. It will continue to be a spot of melancholy interest as long as the ashes of departed saints are deemed of value by the Christian world; and those graves will remain the silent pledges that Burmah will never be abandoned, as a field of missionary exertion, until missionary exertion shall be no longer necessary. The soil in which such choice spirits find rest, the groves in which they seek shelter, the flower which blossoms, and the tree which waves its branches over them, are all sacred in the estimation of those who love God and delight in the glory of his kingdom. Senseless as they are, they assist in forming a shelter for honored dust, over which monuments of marble, with letters of gold and silver, are not worthy to rise. When Mrs. Comstock died another name was added to the glorious catalogue of the fallen — not fallen, but ascended. Another grave was made, from which, on the morning of the resurrection, will come forth a glorified one, to shine in the crown of the Savior forever.

Sarah Davis Comstock was a native of Brookline, Massachusetts. She was the daughter of Robert S. Davis, of the Baptist church in that place. In the house of her father her youthful days were passed, and there she received the mental and moral education which fitted her to labor for the souls of the heathen. In early life she found the Savior, and during her residence in America gave full evidence of a pious, self-denying spirit.

Previous to his sailing for the East, Mr. Comstock selected her for his companion, and with a martyr spirit she determined to bear the sacrifice and endure the toil. She was married to Mr. C., and in the act gave herself not only to him, but to the cause of Christ — to all the sufferings incident to a life in Burmah.

They, in company with several other elected missionaries, were publicly consecrated to the work in June, 1834, and sailed immediately for their field of labor. The services of consecration, on the 28th of June, occurred in the Baldwin Place Church, in

Boston, and were of thrilling interest. Meetings had been held during the day in another church, at which Rev. Mr. Wade and the converts from heathenism, Ko Chet-thing and Moung Sway-moung, had spoken. Indeed, the whole of the previous week had been given to missionary exercises and missionary sympathy; and when the evening of the Sabbath came, the spacious church was densely crowded with an eager and holy throng. Rev. Dr. Wayland delivered an eloquent address of more than an hour's length; after which the missionaries were instructed by Dr. Bolles, secretary of the American Baptist Board, under whose patronage they were to be sent out. When their instructions had been given, Mr. Wade replied in behalf of his brethren and sisters who were so soon to leave our shores. The whole scene was one of deep interest; and many were the prayers offered to God in behalf of that company of devoted Christians. In these delightful services Dr. Comstock, father of Rev. Grover S. Comstock, one of the missionaries, and Rev. Dr. Wisner, secretary of the American Board, participated; and in the crowded house there were several missionaries connected with other denominations, who looked on with thrilling interest and satisfaction. One who witnessed the scene and heard the addresses which were given speaks of the occasion as follows: —

"At seven o'clock, notwithstanding the weather,

that spacious building was crowded to excess, above and below; hundreds were *standing* through the whole service and hundreds retiring from the house because there was not even a place to stand. To be present among those thousands on such an occasion, once in a life, were to stamp that life with an impression to which language is not equal. What, then, must have been felt by each of these missionaries, by their relatives and friends, by those angels who rejoice over one sinner that repenteth, and whose prophetic thoughts would connect this preparatory hour with the repentance of myriads in a distant clime, and age after age?

"We did not wonder, therefore, to hear Dr. Wayland's address open with a confession of the inadequacy of speech to do justice to the thoughts and feelings that fill the soul to overflowing at such an hour. And while listening to his lofty, bold, beautiful, and we may add emphatically *scriptural* delineation of the objects, qualifications, and duties of a Christian missionary, — a delineation that made every other object and character than that of the Christian dwindle into utter insignificance in the comparison, — we felt as did Peter on the mount of glorious vision: 'It is good to be here.' And the thought more than once occurred to us, How would the late venerable Baldwin have enjoyed this scene!

"We were struck by the remark of Mr. Wade,

that, while he regarded the prayers of Christians in this country as indispensable to the success of the mission, he could not but fear that prayers *such as he had sometimes heard* would avail them or their offerers little. The fervor of love, the expectancy of hope, and the persevering constancy of faith were the spiritual qualities wanted. Could they not be obtained?

"In the farewell of Ko Chet-thing and Moung Sway-moung there was a simplicity and pious warmth that went to the heart. They were grateful for the unspeakable blessings of the gospel sent to them when in darkness, and happy alike that they had been permitted of God to see the land where the seed grew; that they were now about to return to plant and rear the tree of the gospel in Burmah; and that they could hope hereafter to meet their Christian friends of America in heaven."

The closing hymn, which was sung by the choir and congregation with fine effect, was written for the occasion by one of the sweetest writers among American poets.

> Native land! — in summer smiling, —
>   Hill and valley, grove and stream;
> Home! whose nameless charms beguiling,
>   Peaceful nursed our infant dream;
> Haunts! to which our childhood hasted,
>   Where the earliest wild flowers grew;
> Church! where Christ's free grace we tasted,
>   Graved on memory's page, — *Adieu!*

Mother! who hast watched our pillow
  In thy tender, sleepless love,
Lo, we dare the crested billow;
  Mother, put thy trust above.
Father! from thy guidance turning,
  O'er the deep our way we take;
Keep the prayerful incense burning
  On thine altar, for our sake.

Brothers! sisters! more than ever
  Are our fond affections twined,
As that hallowed bond we sever
  Which the hand of Nature joined.
But the cry of Burmah's anguish
  Through our inmost hearts doth sound;
Countless souls in misery languish;
  We would fly to heal their wound.

Burmah! we would soothe thy weeping;
  Take us to thy sultry breast;
Where thy sainted dust is sleeping
  Let us share a kindred rest.
Friends! this span of life is fleeting;
  Hark! the harps of angels swell;
Think of that eternal meeting,
  Where no voice shall say, *Farewell!* *

On the morning of Wednesday, July 2, the good ship Cashmere, Captain Hallet, bore them from our shores, some of them to return no more. There were on board Mr. and Mrs. Comstock, Mr. and Mrs. Dean, Mr. and Mrs. Vinton, Mr. and Mrs.

* Mrs. L. H. Sigourney.

Howard, Mr. and Mrs. Wade, Mr. and Mrs. Osgood, Miss Gardener and the Eastern converts, all belonging to the Baptist denomination; together with Dr. Bradley and wife and Miss White, belonging to the stations of the A. B. C. F. M.

The morning dawned in beauty and loveliness; and, as the sun rolled up the sky, a crowd of people were seen assembling on the wharf. Soon from the deck of the vessel was heard the melodious but firm voice of Rev. Dr. Sharp, in prayer to God, pleading for those who were now to commit themselves to the perils of the deep. Hymns were sung, kind words were spoken, Christian greetings were exchanged, and farewell embraces given; and, amid sobs, and tears, and prayers, the vessel swung off from her moorings. As she floated out gently into the harbor the vast crowd on shore commenced singing the hymn of Bishop Heber, —

> "From Greenland's icy mountains,
> From India's coral strand."

This hymn was scarcely finished, and the last echo was yet upon the air, when from the ship was heard another song. Voices which seemed divine united in another hymn, and, as holy stillness gathered over the people, they heard repeated by the departing missionaries the lines of Rev. S. F Smith: —

> "Yes, my native land, I love thee;
> All thy scenes, I love them well."

Such hymns, sung under *such* circumstances, by *such* men and women, must have produced joy and rapture among the ransomed spirits on high; and doubtless Jesus, man's ascended Savior, looked down upon his followers with divine approval.

The Cashmere anchored before Amherst on the 6th of December, and the missionaries were warmly greeted by Dr. Judson and his associates. After remaining a while at Amherst and Maulmain, Mr. Comstock and wife proceeded to the province of Arracan, which was to be the field of their labors; and on the 26th of February, 1835, it being the Sabbath, they performed their first missionary duty in Arracan. On the 4th of March they arrived at Kyouk Phyoo, from which place Mr. Comstock writes an interesting letter, giving a description of the field of labor in which he and his companion were to be engaged. The interest of this sketch will be increased by a perusal of that description in the language of the author himself: —

" As this province is a new field of labor, perhaps a short account of it will not be uninteresting. It is situated on the eastern shore of the Bay of Bengal, and extends from 15° 54′ to 20° 51′ north latitude. Its width is very variable. At the northern part of the province it is about ninety miles wide, while the width at the extreme southern point is but two or three miles. Probably the average width is something less than fifty miles. It is bounded on the north by the Province of Chittagong, on the east by the Burman empire, and on the south and west by the Bay of Bengal. An extensive range of mountains is the boundary between Arracan and Burmah, over which are several passes — one to Ava, one to Prome, another to Bassein, &c. Only the *first* is very much travelled. By this we are only six or eight days' journey from Ava. A good deal of this province is mountainous, and much of the rest is jungle or uncultivated land. The people live in small villages, which are scattered over the whole province. The population, according to the government census, I do not exactly know; but it must be something less than two hundred and fifty thousand. It is very difficult, however, to ascertain the population, as the people will deceive all they can, to avoid taxes, which were very oppressive under the Burman government, and are not very light now. A great deal of itinerant labor must be performed here, as the inhabitants are so scattered; and much must be done by tracts. Two or three laborers besides brother Simons and myself should enter this field as soon as may be. The province is subdivided into four subordinate jurisdictions, called districts. The northern one, Akyab, is the largest. Here is brother Fink, with his native church; and here, I believe, brother Simons intends to settle. The Ramree district is the next in size. It consists of Ramree Island, about forty miles long, and on an average about fifteen wide, extending from 18° 51' to 19° 24' north latitude of Cheduba Island, lying a short distance to the south-west of Ramree, which is eighteen miles long and fourteen wide, and of several smaller islands. There are in the district three hundred and seventy-four villages and about seventy thousand inhabitants. This is the field of labor I occupy. Kyouk Phyoo is on the northern point of Ramree Island; and, though not as central or as large as some other places, is, on some accounts, a very desirable station."

In his labors Mr. C. found a valuable help in Mrs. C., who with unreserved diligence devoted herself to the duties of her station in different parts of Arracan. Though not exposed to the trials and dangers which attended the efforts of the first missionaries, yet in labors abundant and faith unwavering she certainly was.

There is mentioned of her a most beautiful incident which occurred when about to part with her children, who were to visit America to commence a course of instruction not to be obtained in Burmah. When the vessel was about to sail, and Mr. Kincaid, who was to conduct them to this country, was ready to go on board, Mrs. Comstock took her two children and led them forth towards the ocean which would soon part her from them forever, and, kissing the cheek of each, committed them to the care of Him who holds the storms in his hand and controls the tempests as he will. It cost a struggle such only as a mother's heart can feel and realize; and, as she kissed them for the last time and gave them to her husband, she turned her streaming eyes to heaven and exclaimed, " *O Jesus, I do this for thee !* "

It was the last time. The vessel spread her canvas to the gales of heaven, and the children of the devoted woman were wafted from her, to see her face no more; and when next they meet, it will be before the great white throne, where the secrets of all hearts will be revealed, and where the Savior will place upon the head of his servant a crown of glory, and declare, in the hearing of an assembled world, " *This, beloved disciple, I do for thee !* "

It will be a delightful recompense for all the trials, inflictions, and sufferings of a missionary life, and will more than compensate the most self-sacrificing of all earth's children for the most toilsome labors, the most severe trials. Far happier will be he whose brow is encircled with such a crown than he who in this life is hailed as a royal emperor and led in chains of gold from throne to throne, from kingdom to kingdom.

One of our poets has thrown this beautiful incident into rhyme. One verse of his poem we repeat: —

> "One burning kiss, one wild good by;
> Put off, put off from shore!
> In mercy to the mother fly,
> And swiftly waft them from her eye,
> For she can bear no more!
> She knelt and cried, as o'er the sea
> Faded their forms like sunset ray,
> 'O Savior, I do this for thee!'
> And, sobbing, turned away."

The faith of Mrs. Comstock was strong. She believed that the efforts of Christian philanthropy would be attended by the desired blessing, and that Arracan would lift up its hands to God and implore the love of Jesus upon her prostrate sons. In a letter from Ramree, written only a few months before her death, she wrote as follows: "I believe these hills and vales of Arracan will yet leap at the 'sound of the church-going bell,' and the hundreds and thousands of her children will be seen coming up from every city, village, and hamlet, with united heart and voice, to the worship of the great Jehovah. It may not be in my day; but my children *may* see it. God grant that they may be privileged in hastening it on. We see but little fruit of our labors, i. e., so far as converts are concerned, but see the seed germinating. It is not dead — it will yet spring up; yes, this very seed we are now sowing will spring up and yield a glorious harvest."

With this confident expectation she labored on until the hand of death came to close her labors and lead her away to her infinite reward. In whatever part of Arracan she was, she was zealous to do the will of her Master, and seemed governed by a firm determination to glory in nothing but the cross of Jesus. Whether at Kyouk Phyoo, at Akyab, or at Ramree, or any of the other spots of toil and denial, she was *faithful* to the great work assigned her. She never lost sight of the object to accomplish which she had been sent out to a heathen land.

She departed this life on the 28th of April, 1843. Her disease was the malignant dysentery, which is peculiar to the climate. Her two children, lovely little boys, followed her to the grave; and in three months they were laid to rest by her side. About two hundred inhabitants of the Ramree district attended her funeral; and when the disconsolate husband had gone to his deserted home they remained and poured forth their sorrow over the new-made grave. Her death exerted a deep and powerful influence on the minds of the natives; and some were led to prepare to meet God by seeking the mercy of his Son.

The touching account of the death of his companion we give in Mr. C.'s own words: " For several months past Mrs. Comstock had been blessed with unusually good health; and we had repeatedly spoken with gratitude of the goodness of God in granting us so long an exemption from sickness.

We hoped, too, that we should be permitted to labor more vigorously and uninterruptedly for the good of the heathen than we had been able to do. She had just completed a Book for Mothers, which, I think, was greatly needed, and will, I trust, prove very useful. She was contemplating a work for children, and had begun to inquire for scholars to attend during the rains, just at hand. We had, too, already decided to spend a month or two early in the cold season at Cheduba, and then take a tour of a month to Ava and the villages on the way thither. Our prospects for the future appeared to be unusually encouraging; and we fondly hoped that we should be permitted to see many turning unto the Lord in Arracan. We did not, however, forget that death might destroy all our plans, and often conversed together freely on the probability that one of us might be called speedily into eternity. She had no fear of death nor any anxiety as to the time or manner of her departure, but only spoke of it as affecting our future course.

"She was taken ill on Saturday, April 22. Our English doctor was then absent from Ramree; but, had he been here, we should not, probably, have thought it necessary to call him, as Mrs. C. had prescribed for many similar cases with entire success. On Monday I saw that her disease was very severe and obstinate, and asked her if I had not better call the Mussulman doctor who is left in charge here when the English one is absent. He came Tuesday morning. He prescribed for her, but wished the English doctor sent for; and I despatched a messenger for him. He arrived early on Wednesday morning, and faithfully and assiduously tried every remedy to arrest the disease, but in vain. On Friday evening, the 28th, at eight o'clock, she very suddenly expired. Occasionally there were slight symptoms of amendment; and I fondly hoped, to the very last, that she might recover. A minute or two before her death she took some nourishment, and remarked that she thought she should soon regain her strength. I trusted that it might be so, and stepped on to the veranda to say to the native Christians that there was still a little reason to hope. I heard her speak, and hastened to her just in time to see her sink back upon her pillow, and, without a struggle or even a gasp, breathe her last.

" The body was immediately surrounded by weeping and wailing heathen women, who felt that they had lost a friend. Such indeed was the case; for Mrs. C. truly pitied and loved the women of Arracan, and was never happier than when telling them of the Savior. On the day after her death, as the news spread in the town, men, women, and children (more of the last two) began to crowd to my house; and it was estimated that about two thousand were here during the day. Their expressions of attachment to my dear wife and of sorrow for her loss were deeply affecting. 'How kindly she always spoke to me when she met me!' 'She always gave us medicine when we were sick.' 'She was truly a good woman.' 'She came here to die, far from her native land, with no mother or sister near her, because she pitied us.' Expressions similar to these were made and listened to with many tears. I remarked once, 'What crowds are pressing to the house! Are *all* from the town?' A bystander replied, 'Yes; as the news spreads all will be here, for she was greatly beloved.' Another added 'Many tears will be shed in Ramree to-day.'

"I was surprised and deeply affected to witness such manifestations of feeling among the heathen towards a Christian missionary. They more firmly convinced me that she had not lived in vain, but had exerted an extensive and salutary influence, which, I doubt not, will be powerfully felt in preparing the way of the Lord here. Her labors, too, I trust, will prove the means of salvation to many souls. She was a most conscientious and laborious missionary. The rains before last she had a school, to which she devoted a good deal of time; translated the Scripture Catechism, administered medicine to the sick, conversed with the women who were daily calling at the house, and taught her own children, besides attending to household duties. She was from daylight till nine o'clock at evening constantly engrossed with labors and cares. As far as her own feelings were concerned, she would have delighted uniformly to be as active and busy as she then was.

"She was not, however, always called to such constant and severe labor, but uniformly did what she could. Whenever women came to the house she felt it her duty to leave all and go and tell them of the Savior; and I recollect that in a few instances, when she was so engaged that she could not at once go to them, and they left without hearing of Christ, she was very much grieved on account of it. If I was not at hand, she conversed with the men, too. Towards evening, when she could be out, she might often be found seated on a rice mortar, with half a dozen women around her, in the adjoining villages. Attention to the sick, also, demanded a good deal of her time and thought. I have known her to give medicine to twenty applicants in a day. She was always anxious to accompany me in my tours to the villages during the cold season; but circumstances usually prevented it. She would have prepared more works for the press but for a feeling of extreme self-depreciation, which led her to think that she was not competent to prepare a book fit to be printed. The Scripture Catechism and Mother's Book are both, I think, calculated to do much good. She not only labored faithfully, but prayed fervently, and with tears, for the salvation of the heathen. She has, however entered into her rest; her labors and prayers have ceased; and I am left alone to train my children up for God and to do what I can to win the heathen to Christ. The Lord has thus decided; and he does all things well. I am enabled to say, in sincerity I trust, 'Thy will be done.' I have lost a most affectionate and amiable wife, my children have lost a kind and faithful mother, and a prayerful and diligent laborer is lost to the cause of missions; but I will not repine or murmur. The Lord is as rich in mercy as he is infinite in wisdom; and let him do what seemeth good in his sight. I need not ask the sympathy and prayers for the members of the Board and other friends, for I feel assured that I shall have them. Pray, not only that my affliction may be greatly sanctified to my spiritual good and to the good of other friends and other missionaries, but also that the death of my dear wife may be made the means of life to many souls in Arracan. Several appear tender, and seem to recall the instructions she has given them."

Mr. Comstock did not long survive her. In about one year from the time his wife was taken from her toils his earthly joys and sorrows closed, and he went up on high. Borne down by anxiety, care, and affliction, he died April 24, 1844. He was the third son of Rev. Oliver C. Comstock, of Michigan. He graduated at Hamilton Institution in 1827.

For a while he studied and practised law in the city of Rochester, where he was becoming very successful as a counsellor. But God had another station for him to occupy — a wide field of usefulness for him to fill. In the winter of 1831 he was led to view himself as a sinner and embrace Jesus as his Savior. He became a member of the First Baptist Church, and was baptized by his venerated father. Soon he became convinced that the Christian ministry demanded his exertions and powers. He soon removed to Hamilton and entered the theological class, and at once commenced preparing himself for labors in Burmah, and soon went forth to do the will of God in wild and uncultivated regions. But his afflictions were many — his toils great — his years few. He died ere the desire of his heart had been realized. He ascended to heaven ere the field given him to cultivate was seen blossoming as the rose.

Called by God, he left the path to earthly honor and distinction and entered the scorned and despised service of the crucified One, and in that service found an early grave. He saw his beloved companion go down to the tomb; he saw two darling babes laid beside her; and, panting for the loved ones, he himself went down into the sepulchre.

Here ends the record of a family sacrificed on the altar of Christian benevolence; a record written with tears of sorrow and anguish, yet gleaming with signs of glory; a record which even the cold cynic might respect, and the stoic read with emotions of wonder and admiration.

> " Patriots have toiled, and in their country's cause
> Bled nobly; and their deeds, as they deserve,
> Receive proud recompense. We give in charge
> Their names to the sweet lyre. The Historic Muse,
> Proud of the treasure, marches with it down
> To latest times; and Sculpture, in her turn,
> Gives bond in stone and ever-during brass
> To guard them and immortalize her trust.
> But fairer wreaths are due, though never paid,
> To those who, posted at the shrine of **Truth**,
> **Have** fallen in her defence."

CHAPTER VIII.

HENRIETTA SHUCK,

OF CHINA.

THE Celestial empire has become an object of great interest. Its vast extent, its swarming inhabitants, its peculiar customs, its steady resistance of modern inventions, and its obstinate defiance of Christianity, all draw upon it the gaze of the Christian world. The time was when China was barred and bolted against the truth; when on her soil could be found no teacher of the true faith: when a high wall separated the ignorant inhabitants from the rest of the world. But the wall has been thrown down; the obstacles in the way of Christianity have in many cases been removed; and China is open to the footsteps of the man of God.

Following the leadings of divine Providence, good men of various denominations have planted mission stations within the hallowed enclosures of the proud monarch of that great empire, and in the midst of superstition and abomination planted the saving cross.

The station to which Mrs. Shuck belonged was under the control of the Baptist Missionary Convention. It was at Macao, a beautiful peninsula, four miles in length, peopled with about forty thousand Chinese and Portuguese. Mrs. Shuck describes the climate as delightful and the situation of the place beautifully romantic. Though destitute of many of the dear associations connected with stations in and about Palestine, yet to a mind like that of Mrs. S. there was much in the wild beauty of the scenery and the strange customs of the people to interest and please; and all her letters give evidence that in that spot she found a home where she could labor with pleasure to herself and profit to others around her.

But she was not destined to spend all her days at Macao. The providence of God soon suggested a removal to Hong Kong, forty miles east of Macao. Her own health seemed to require such a step, as the unprotected state of the peninsula was fast wearing her into the grave. Certain advantageous offers were also made, and a prospect of increased usefulness presented to her husband; and in 1842 Mr. Shuck bade farewell to his old field of labor, and entered upon one where the prospect of success was much more abundant.

The maiden name of Mrs. Shuck was Henrietta

Hall. Her father was Rev. Addison Hall, a faithful, devoted minister of the gospel. Her mother was daughter of Colonel Elias Edmonds, of Virginia. They were both remarkable for intelligence and piety, and were universally esteemed. They were members of the Moratico Baptist Church, having been received by Rev. S. L. Straughan.

On the 28th of October, 1817, Henrietta was born in the beautiful little village of Kilmarnock, but a few miles from the rolling waves of Chesapeake Bay. Her early days were spent near this beautiful spot, where she was known as a frank, amiable, kind-hearted girl. Her youth was passed with her parents, who exerted themselves to expand her mind and improve her heart. To the fond hearts of the parents she was an object of tender solicitude and care, and they longed to see her brought to the feet of the Lord Jesus.

In 1831 extensive revivals were enjoyed throughout the country, and in these revivals Virginia largely shared. It was during this year that Miss Hall was converted. A camp meeting was being held near her birthplace, in which her father was much interested; and feeling that moral and religious training was much more important than intellectual culture, he sent for his daughter, who was attending school at Fredericksburg, to return home and enjoy the privileges of the work of grace. She came, not thinking of the change which was soon to take place in her moral character. Young and happy, she put far off the evil day; and the awful conviction that she was a sinner had not produced any serious impression upon her mind. But God's hand was in her timely return, and his grace had marked her as one of its choicest subjects. She no sooner commenced attending the meeting than she began to feel the force of truth and hear the voice of the Spirit and the monitions of the Holy Ghost. Under the solemn presentation of the sinner's lost condition, young Henrietta began to realize that she was lost without a Savior. The fact was before her mind day and night, and she found no rest. True, she had lived on earth but a short time, and, when compared with others, had committed but few sins; but these few were aggravated and overwhelming. God she had not loved; Christ she had not embraced. She had violated the wise and holy law of the universe, and, to complete the work of woe, had rejected the blood of the Son of God. She had a view of sin as God presents it in his word; and when she saw *herself* as a sinner, the contemplation was crushing and terrible. But these feelings of deep anguish did not long continue. God heard her cries of penitence, and for the sake of Christ forgave all the past, and caused joy, like a deep, strong tide, to flow into her soul. Her rapture was as ecstatic as her sorrow had been oppressive; and on the listening ear of her sister penitents she poured the story of her change from death to life.

She was baptized on the 2d of September, 1831, by Rev. J. B. Jeter. It was a holy spectacle. The youthful candidate for the sublime ordinance was not yet fourteen years of age; and, as she descended the bank and entered the flood, a deep and awful silence gathered over the crowded shores. The voice of mirth and profanity was hushed; and to many a heart came the spirit tone, "This is the way; walk ye in it." As she came up out of the water a cheerful smile was seen playing upon her countenance, which told of sweet and precious peace and delightful communion with her Maker. The pastor who administered the ordinance, the church which received her to its fellowship, the anxious parents, have had no reason to regret the important step then taken; and though they must have seen her baptized with fear and trembling lest she should in her youth be deceived and eventually return to the cold and heartless service of the world, yet they commended her to that Being who is able and faithful to keep all who are committed to his care. Nor did the world with its curling lip and contemptuous tone ever tell how the youthful disciple witnessed a good profession and afterwards denied it.

A few months after her baptism Henrietta was called to part with her beloved mother, who died in

December of the same year. To the young Christian this bereavement was full of sorrow and full of blessing. While it deprived her of a mother's counsels and prayers, while it took from her one to whom she had looked for maternal sympathy and encouragement, it taught her the uncertainty of life, threw her more upon herself and on her Savior, placed a greater weight of care upon her, and thus fitted her for the duties which she afterwards performed so faithfully as a missionary of the cross.

In the early part of 1835, or the latter part of the year preceding, Miss Hall became acquainted with her future husband, who had recently decided to become a missionary in the East. He made, with an offer of marriage, the proposal of a missionary life. She had not then reached her eighteenth year, and was a young, freehearted girl, who knew but little of toil or anxiety. Her extreme youth caused her to hesitate; and she accepted the proposal only when it appeared to be a solemn and imperious duty. Her mind wandered forward to the parting with her dear parent and other fond friends; to the tender farewell at sailing; to long years of labor, perhaps of suffering, in China; to a rude home there, and perhaps a grave. Then followed the prospect of usefulness; the hope of saving souls from death and doing a work of benevolence on soil not before cultivated by the Christian laborer. And perhaps with these were some vague and romantic notions about a missionary life and a missionary home. Youth is fond of new and strange objects; and our heroine doubtless became attracted by the novelty and romance of the life she was to live. Strange were it not so in the ardor and inexperience of youthful piety; and the fact that romance casts its sombre shadow over the pious missionary female, as she leaves home and native land, detracts but little from the admiration with which we gaze upon her lofty career. The oldest, most prudent, man seldom fails of being interested in such enterprises by their novelty; and should we cast away all around whom it gathers its strange witchery, few would be left to toil for human good. He who moves above all such motives must have a mind perfectly trained and a heart perfectly alive to the glory of God. After a due consideration of the subject, Miss Hall decided to go forth a servant of her Master. She was married to Rev. J. Lewis Shuck on the 8th of September, 1835. The service was performed by Rev. H. Keeling, in the city of Richmond. On the 10th Mr. S. and Rev. R. D. Davenport were consecrated to the work of God in one of the Baptist churches in the same city, and soon after embarked for Boston, one to sail for China and the other for Siam. The vessel in which passage had been engaged for Mr. and Mrs. Shuck was the Louvre, which was to carry out a large delegation of missionaries. They sailed on the 22d of September, a beautiful day, on which Nature seemed to have bestowed her charms in profusion. On board were eleven ordained ministers, who were leaving home to do good in distant lands. Among these was Rev. Howard Malcom, D. D., who went out at the request of the Baptist Triennial Convention to visit the stations of that denomination and advise and encourage the toilers in the East. The large number of ministers on board, one of them having long been an esteemed pastor of a flourishing church, drew together an immense crowd of pious people, who came to exchange parting tokens and give the parting hand to the faithful brethren and sisters who were about to fulfil the command of our ascended Savior — " Go ye into all the world and preach the gospel to every creature." The wharf was crowded with people; and the rigging of vessels in the harbor was filled with strong men, who looked with strange feelings upon a sight the like of which is seldom witnessed. The hour arrived. The ship swung off from her moorings and floated down the harbor. One sail after another was thrown out to the breath of heaven; and in beautiful style the vessel was borne onward and soon lost from sight. The spectators slowly and sadly returned to their homes, praying the God of ocean and storm to keep the precious cargo safe from danger.

To Mrs. S. the voyage was not a pleasant one. A violent seasickness commenced as soon as she left the Harbor of Boston and continued a long time. This was succeeded by sickness of other kinds, and the whole voyage was spent in suffering. In her published letters to her friends she gives thrilling descriptions of her sorrow, and declares that while she did not dream of half the suffering which she had experienced, yet the same voyage would she take again, were there no other way to reach her field of labor. Admirable woman! Worn down with sickness and scarcely able to hold the pen, she writes the sentence at a time when we would suppose she would be shrinking back and ready to faint.

On the 4th of February, 1836, anchor was cast at Kedgeree, nearly a hundred miles below Calcutta. At night they all disembarked and for the first time slept on heathen soil. From Kedgeree they sailed along to Amherst, where sleep the forms of Mrs. Judson and her babe in the silence of the grave. What were the feelings of Mrs. Shuck as she stood there over the spot so dear to every pious heart, or plucked a small branch of the "hopia tree" to send home to her sire, we do not know; but doubtless her mind was filled with sad forebodings and awful thoughts. "Am I to sleep in such a grave? be buried away from home, with such a tree as this to wave over me?" "Am I to fall in China, and see my friends no more? Have I looked upon the shores of America for the last time?" Questions like these must have been suggested to her as she stood with her husband beside the grave of Burmah's proto-martyr.

After stopping a while at Maulmain and Singapore, the missionaries arrived at Macao in November, 1836, and here commenced immediate preparation to engage in the gospel work. Their first son was born shortly before their arrival at Macao. They called him Lewis, for his father. On the 29th of October the second son was born, who was named Ryland Keeling. With these two babes around her, the labor of the mother was materially increased and essentially changed. Her own family required more of her care, and gave her less time and opportunity to do good abroad. Yet, with her family as it was, she is said to have found much time for the usual purposes of missionary life, and was zealously engaged in plans for the spiritual improvement of those around her.

While at Macao her heart was cheered by hearing that God was pouring out his Spirit in her own dear land; that he was converting sinners, and among them some who had been her intimate friends. Her own sisters were led to give their hearts to God; and when the intelligence crossed the deep, and was told in the hearing of tne sad and perhaps almost discouraged missionary, her joy knew no bo nds. It was as a cup of cold water to one dying with thirst; and the letter which brought the tidings was read over and over again, and frequently bathed in tears of joy. Her letters to her sisters express her deep interest in their spiritual welfare. She pleads with them by the love of Jesus that they be faithful to the Savior of their souls and walk worthy of Him who has bought them with his own blood. To do this, she urges them to study the word of God, and be constant in the closet, and meditate much upon spiritual things, and watch and guard the heart from temptation and sin. Nor does she forget to recommend the cultivation of a missionary spirit, but, with all the eloquence of a sister's love, urges them to do good as they have opportunity.

In January, 1837, Mr. Shuck baptized the first man who had been converted through his agency. His name was Ah Loo.* For about a year previous

---

The baptism of Ah Loo is thus described by Mr. Shuck: "At seven o'clock this evening we repaired to the water; and although the natural sun was not permitted to attest this first baptismal scene in China, yet the effulgence of the Sun of Righteousness shone upon us; and if ever we felt his genial rays, it was then. Contrary to our expectations, we did not go half so far as we anticipated, but stopped upon the beach at a suitable place, within a few rods of a large Portuguese fort with mounted ramparts. Here, in broken sentences, we united our hearts in prayer to God that he would forgive our weakness and many imperfections, and grant us his smile and heavenly grace now and during our whole lives. Then handing my cap and cane to Mrs. Shuck, who stood on the bank, the only earthly witness of the joyful event, I had the privilege of burying with Christ in baptism this willing convert from heathenism, being the first Chinese that was ever baptized within the confines of this vast and idolatrous empire."

to his baptism he lived as cook in the mission family. During the year he became greatly attached to those whom he served, and would let no opportunity pass without showing his gratitude. They, of course, instructed him in the principles of the Christian religion. He was a willing learner, and soon gave evidence of being a changed, regenerated man. Yet the missionary was cautious, and for a long time held back his disciple; but at length, convinced of the genuineness of his conversion, led him down into the flowing tide and baptized him. This event was an occasion of great joy to our sister, who, with her husband, had done so much to enlighten the poor idolatrous Chinaman. Ah Loo maintained a constant walk for a long time; but at length, temptation proving too powerful for him, he was overcome, and sinned against God. This fall was full of sorrow to the missionaries, as his conversion had been full of joy and hope; and when the news came that he had disgraced his high profession and wronged his blessed Savior, they bowed their hearts in sadness, and prayed to Heaven that the wanderer might yet be restored and the straying child brought back to the Father's arms.

In 1841 Mrs. Shuck gave birth to a beautiful little daughter, who was called Henrietta Layton, for her mother, and a family by the latter name who had been exceeding kind to them during all their residence at Macao. To justify her course in conferring this name instead of one selected from her numerous friends in America, she relates numberless instances of kindness on the part of the family alluded to; instances of kindness without which the missionary family would have been put to considerable inconvenience and perhaps acute suffering. In 1842 Mr. Shuck removed to Hong Kong. The providence of God clearly indicated this as the path of duty; and though the separation with pleasant acquaintances at Macao was trying, the step was cheerfully taken. A beautiful spot was selected for a chapel, and money raised with which to erect it; and the divine blessing manifestly attended every step. To complete the work, Mr. Shuck made great sacrifices and practised great self-denial. He employed his own funds, expended his own means, to complete the work; and deemed it no sacrifice, though he was often deprived of the comforts of life. He was well aware that God would prosper him; and though he knew not how, he rested in the confident hope that he would ultimately receive at the hand of God far more than he had expended n his service.

The health of Mrs. S., instead of improving, seemed to fail at Hong Kong, and no means which were taken could restore it. Physicians were consulted and journeys made, but all to no purpose. The hand of disease was laid heavily upon her sinking system; and day by day her eye became more dim and her cheek more bloodless. Still she labored on, and counted it her meat and drink to do the will of her divine Master. Her language was, —

> " Shall I be carried to the skies
> On flowery beds of ease,
> While others fought to win the prize
> And sailed through bloody seas ? "

Mrs. S., according to her biographer, seemed to have premonitions of her death. For a whole year previous to the occurrence of the event the conviction was deepening in her mind that her race was well nigh run and her days nearly finished. The idea that *something* was soon to arrive, and that something to be of importance to her, weighed upon her mind. Filled with emotions which such a presentiment was calculated to produce, she made preparation for the grave. She endeavored to have her family arrangements made so that she could depart at a moment's notice. She was also led to prayer and self-consecration; and her heart, as well as her family arrangements, was in order. The premonitions which many persons suppose they have are generally the results of an excited fancy, and as often prove false as true. Every person may find in his or her daily life many events which appear mysterious; and should importance be attached to them, we should be rendered miserable. Many are alarmed at the breaking of a mirror the crowing of a bird at midnight, the sudden extinguishing of a lamp by the wind, and other things equally as simple. These common occurrences are to them omens of approaching evil, and they allow them to have all the influence of rea.ity. Whether they prove true or false, they are sources to the superstitious of unhappiness. With Mrs. S. there appeared to be an indefinable impression, which might have arisen from the precarious state of her health and from the fact that the period of her fifth confinement was rapidly hastening, and it was doubtful if she could endure the trials of such an occurrence in her weak and debilitated condition. But, whatever may have been the cause of her forebodings, they were acted upon as facts; and had she known of her death with absolute certainty, she could not have made more temporal and spiritual preparation for it.

At three o'clock on the morning of the 27th of November, 1844, she died. The evening previous to her death was spent in prayer with her husband and children. Early on the night of the 26th, the long-expected and dreaded event announced itself by the premonitory symptoms. The physician was summoned, and the dear friends anxiously awaited the result. But nature was unable to sustain the fearful burden imposed upon it, and gradually gave way until the hour mentioned, when the spirit was released and all was over.

> "Vital spark of heavenly flame,
> Quit, O, quit this mortal frame;
> Trembling, hoping, lingering, flying,
> O, the pain, the bliss, of dying!
> Cease, fond nature, cease thy strife,
> And let me languish into life."

It was hard for the husband to give up his companion under such trying circumstances, and harder still to have her die without the utterance of a single expression; but who that knew her life would doubt the character of the thoughts which crowded thick and fast upon her mind as the time of her departure was at hand? Religion was her life; and the last words she uttered were of high and holy import. A few hours before she died she called her husband to her couch and asked him to kneel in prayer. He did so, and to every expression of love to Jesus she responded by the warm pressure of his hand. We cannot doubt the evidence which such a saint gives; and though the last hour may be spent in a silence which nothing disturbs but the sobs of friends, we can leave the cold clay in the tomb, with the sweet consolation of *knowing* that the ransomed spirit has fled to a land of holy rest. We can say, —

> "How blest the righteous when she dies,
> When sinks a weary soul to rest!
> How mildly beam the closing eyes!
> How gently heaves th' expiring breast!"

The funeral of Mrs. Shuck was attended from her late home, and she was borne to the grave by the European police corps, who volunteered their services for the occasion. There have been cases in which missionary women have died and had only *one* to follow them to the grave. On some occasions the husband has prepared the shroud, made the coffin, dug the grave, and followed the corpse to the tomb, accompanied only by a weeping, motherless child, or by the unseen One, who said, "Lo, I am with you always, even unto the end." But on this occasion there were many mourners. A large company followed to the grave in which her remains were placed. The religious service on the occasion was performed by Rev. Mr. Devan. At the grave Rev. Mr. Brown offered prayer and made appropriate remarks to the crowd who assembled.

Thus mysteriously departed on the passage of death a most worthy and beloved wife, a fond mother, and a faithful Christian. There were many circumstances connected with her death to make it a sad one. Her husband was not the only sufferer by the dreadful bereavement. Five motherless children were left among strangers in a strange land; and from many who had experienced her kindness went up a wail of lamentation over her early grave.

One who knew her well, and who labored for

Jesus and the dying heathen in the same land,' writes of her as follows: " She was married to Rev. Mr. Shuck in 1835, and in September of the same year sailed with her husband, in company with a large number of missionaries, for the East. They remained in Singapore four months, where their eldest son was born, and in September, 1836, arrived in China. They remained in Macao till March, 1842, when they removed to Hong Kong. While at Macao they were allowed to prosecute the study of language, the instruction of youth, and teaching the people. On their arrival at Hong Kong they were prepared to renew their labors on an enlarged scale and without restraint. Chapels were erected, assemblies collected, and schools gathered from the Chinese; and while her husband labored among the former, Mrs. Shuck instructed the latter. She possessed considerable knowledge of the written language, and still greater familiarity with the colloquial of the Chinese, and devoted joyfully and successfully her acquirements, time, and talents to the interests of the mission. During the last year of her life a new school house had been erected and a school gathered under her care, of twenty Chinese boys and six girls, besides her own four children; making, in all, thirty under her supervision. In this work she took the greatest

* Rev. William Dean.

interest, and all the time and strength which could be spared from the care of her family and the culture of her own children were joyfully devoted to the nstruction of the children of the heathen. Her prospects of usefulness had never been greater, and her heart had never been more encouraged, than during the last year of her life. But in the midst of her highest hopes, while children were seeking instruction, the heathen were inquiring the way to Christ, and the general prospects of the mission were brightening, and herself in comfortable health and active life, she was cut down in a single night, and her family overwhelmed with grief and the mission again overshadowed with gloom.

"Under the influence of a secret conviction that her end was near, she had 'set her house in order,' and was prepared for the event; while, at the same time, she prosecuted her daily duties with her accustomed cheerfulness, and laid out plans for labor which would have required a long life to perform.

"It is a matter of devout gratitude to the wise Disposer of all events, that, just before the death of Mrs. Shuck, her particular friends, Dr. and Mrs. Devan, should become members of her family; and now the five motherless children may find in Mrs. Devan one so well qualified and so sincerely desirous of supplying, to the extent of her power, their irreparable loss. Mrs. D. will also act as the superintendent of the school for Chinese children. The friends of the mission will unite their prayers that life may be preserved and health and grace may be adequate to the responsibilities and duties of the station she is by such a mysterious and painful providence so unexpectedly called to occupy.

"Mrs. Shuck left her father's house and native land in her eighteenth year, and, by thus giving the freshness of her youth to the cause of Christ and the good of the heathen, has left us the best proof of the purity of her faith and the sincerity of her piety. During her eight years' residence in China she has done much for the happiness of her family and to aid her husband in his work, besides giving much direct instruction to those around her. Her house was ever open to the stranger, and her heart ever sympathized with the needy and afflicted, and her hands were diligently employed in acts of kindness and charity."

Let us now draw the veil over the scene, and bow our hearts to the superior wisdom of Him who cannot err; and, while we lament for the early fallen, may we pray the Lord of the harvest to send forth new laborers into his vineyard. The heathen are not yet converted, the world is not yet redeemed, the throne of Satan is not yet overturned.

Impressed by the terrible aspect of the world, let the contemplation of missionary biography urge us on to missionary labors and missionary piety, until the voice of joy and praise shall resound from pole to pole.

CHAPTER IX.

SARAH B. JUDSON,

OF BURMAH.

RALPH and Abiah Hall lived in quiet Alstead, New Hampshire. On the morning of November 4, 1803, their first child was born. They named her Sarah, in memory of a deceased relative. While in her youth the parents removed from New Hampshire to Massachusetts, and established themselves in Salem, where the younger days of our subject were spent. Of her childhood but little can be said. She was like other children, and spent her time in a childish manner; and connected with her early years were but few circumstances of any special interest.

Up to her sixteenth year she seems to have had but few convictions of sin. The great subject of the soul's salvation, if presented at all, made slight impression upon her mind and heart. The warnings and invitations of the gospel were alike unheeded, and she lived until this period in sinful thoughtlessness. In 1820 she found hope in the Savior, and on the 4th of June made a public profession of religion, and in the presence of a great congregation gave herself away to God and to his people. The solemn, awful step she fully realized; and when she was led down into her baptismal sepulchre, and buried there, her heart was fully given up to God. The venerable and departed Dr. Bolles administered the ordinance, and received her by the impressive rite of "fellowship" to the First Baptist Church in Salem, of which he was then pastor.

At that time the missionary spirit was beginning to pervade the churches of America and exert its holy influence upon the minds of the members. Young Sarah Hall caught the holy enthusiasm. Just converted, fresh from the public vows of consecration, the anxious question, "Lord, what wilt thou have me to do?" upon her lips, she was in the exact frame of mind best adapted to be moulded by holy zeal for a dying race.

The feelings which struggled in her soul found utterance through the columns of the Christian Watchman in various prose and poetic effusions. These articles do not exhibit any extraordinary poetic merit. They hardly do credit to her real abilities. Bearing the marks of haste, these early productions never gave any peculiar pleasure to the authoress; but for deep feeling and pathos they are remarkable. They seem to be the outgushings of a soul stirred up with holy enthusiasm and flowing out in channels of its own formation. She evidently wrote, not for the severity of the critic, but for the warm heart of the Christian; not to awaken feelings of admiration, but to kindle up the flame of divine animation; not to win fame for herself, but to inspire others with love for the perishing.

One of these poems was the instrument in bringing her into an acquaintance with George D. Boardman, her future husband. The poem was upon the death of Coleman, whose fall in a distant land, ere he had buckled the armor on, produced feelings of sadness in the hearts of all American Christians. Boardman saw it, and his soul was moved by it. Who the writer was he did not know, but determined to discover, if possible, what heart kept time with the wild beatings of his own. The first verse of that poem runs as follows:—

> " 'Tis the voice of deep sorrow from India's shore;
>   The flower of our churches is withered, is dead!
> The gem that shone brightly will sparkle no more,
>   And the tears of the Christian profusely are shed.
> Two youths of Columbia, with hearts glowing warm,
>   Embarked on the billows far distant to rove,
> To bear to the nations all wrapped in thick gloom
>   The lamp of the gospel — the message of love.
> But Wheelock now slumbers beneath the cold wave;
> And Coleman lies low in the dank, cheerless grave:

> Mourn, daughters of Arracan, mourn!
> The rays of that star, clear and bright,
> That so sweetly on Chittagong shone,
> Are shrouded in black clouds of night;
> For Coleman is gone!"

Mr. Boardman at once determined to discover the writer of these thrilling lines, and in a short time was enabled to trace them to the pen of Miss Hall. Ere he had seen her who was to be the companion of his arduous labors, the sharer of his success, and the attendant of his dying bed, he seems to have sought for the youthful authoress with a kind of intuition that God had fitted her to be his companion. Nor was he disappointed on an acquaintance with his young friend. He found her in possession of an active mind, a warm heart, and an agreeable person. He made proposals to her immediately, and requested her company to the heathen world. To such an enterprise all her friends were averse. To Mr. Boardman they had no objection; but the idea of sending out the flower of their family to wither and die on heathen soil they could not endure. The parents were oppressed with sorrow at what they considered the wild and romantic notions of their child, and for a long time withheld all consent, and steadfastly resisted every movement towards a missionary life. And when the daughter did gain their permission, it came like water wrung from the solid rock. These pious people did not understand the claim which God has upon the services of all his children; they did not understand the honor and glory of having a child in heathen lands laboring for the salvation of the dying; they did not know what a halo of light would in after years be thrown around the name of her who was about to embark on the perilous voyage; and when she left them they looked upon her as buried out of their sight.

Probably much of Miss Hall's enthusiasm in the missionary work was caught from Mrs. Judson, who visited this country in 1823. They became acquainted shortly after the arrival of Mrs. J., and continued correspondence as long as she remained in America; and when she sailed forth again, to return no more, no prayer of greater fervency was offered for her safety and success than was breathed forth by young Sarah Hall, who was so soon to follow her illustrious example in scenes of trial and self-devotion.

George D. Boardman and Sarah Hall were married in Salem, by Rev. Lucius Bolles, D. D., on the 3d day of July, 1825. Her personal appearance was good. Though not positively handsome, her countenance was agreeable and prepossessing. She usually wore a pleasant smile; and an air of frankness and ingenuous openness was a peculiar characteristic. She was affable and courteous, with sufficient dignity and grace. We may, however, suppose her husband to have been more attracted by her intellect and heart than by the outward ornament of person.

The vessel which conveyed Mr. and Mrs. Boardman to the "shades of moral death" sailed from Boston in 1825; and in due time the missionaries arrived in Calcutta. Here they remained nearly two years, employed in missionary work and doing good as they had opportunity. On the 17th of April, 1827, they entered Amherst, and found there the grave of Ann H. Judson and the bending form of her bereaved husband. That good man's trials were not at an end. His dear daughter Maria was dying; and Boardman's own hand formed her little coffin, and dug her grave, and supported the trembling form of the father, when his child, the daughter of the sainted mother and wife, was laid to rest.

While at Calcutta, the union of husband and wife was cemented by the birth of the first child — a daughter, whom they called Sarah Ann. The occurrence of this event, while it withdrew the devoted mother from the labors and toils of her missionary life, awakened in her bosom feelings which had never been stirred there before. A new world of thought and action was before her mind; and, to use her own language, she "was another creature." On his arrival at Amherst Boardman conferred with the other missionaries, who, after mature deliberation, advised him to commence labors at Maulmain.

about twenty-five miles from Amherst, to which place he proceeded with his little family. Soon a bamboo house was erected for him, and his work of self-denial and suffering commenced. They were annoyed in various ways by the natives, and several times were plundered by the hordes of robbers that descended from the mountains at night and assaulted every dwelling which promised considerable booty. Their house was pillaged in this manner but a short time after they arrived at Maulmain. One night they went to sleep as usual, after committing themselves to the care of Him whose eyes are never closed to sleep. Awaking at midnight, Mrs. B. found the lamp, which had been left burning, extinguished, and in the dim moonlight the furniture of the room appeared to be in confusion. To light the lamp was but the work of a moment, on which a fearful scene was presented. Every thing of value had been taken away, and all that remained was in terrible confusion. During this robbery Mr. Boardman was painfully awake to every thing which transpired; while his wife, wearied with toil, slept as sweetly as if the villains who had caused such havoc had been kind attendants on errands of mercy. And providential was it that she did not awake. While some were carrying away the property, others stood over the prostrate forms of the sleeping family, ready to murder them if they awoke. Boardman knew it all — he knew hat fierce eyes were watching him — that the uplifted weapon was ready to drink his blood. A single movement on the part of the sleepers would have brought down that weapon and hurried them from the scene of their labors to the bar of Him who had sent them forth to do his work, declaring, "Lo, I am with you alway."

In the early part of 1828 it was deemed advisable for Mr. Boardman to remove to Tavoy, about one hundred and fifty miles south of Maulmain; and, in accordance with certain instructions from the Board, he took up his residence there in April. On his arrival he found the "whole city given to idolatry." On every hand were the melancholy evidences of heathen worship, heathen superstition, and heathen cruelty. Gaudama was worshipped by all the people, and upwards of two hundred priests ministered at the various temples. The faithful missionary commenced his labors immediately on his arrival: his zayat went up within sight of the great pagoda, and daily he sat at the door to instruct the passing population. While at Tavoy, Mrs. Boardman was employed with her domestic duties, and with the instruction of the children who could be gathered into the school, which was commenced on their arrival. We deem the cares of one's own family enough to employ all the time of a female in this country; but the labors of Mrs. B., in her feeble state of health, were augmented, not merely by the children of the boarding school, but also by the care and instruction of the school itself. Uncomplainingly she performed her arduous labors, while day after day her health grew poorer and her cheek paler. It was at Tavoy that Ko Thah-byu was "buried with Christ by baptism." In his early days he had been a very wicked man. His path was stained with blood, and to all around he gave evidence of his ferocious, bloodthirsty nature. He was converted at Maulmain, and removed with Mr. B. to Tavoy. After his baptism he was a most faithful and devoted laborer. His nature seemed to be entirely changed. From being one of the most ferocious and dreadful tyrants, he became gentle, humble, forgiving, and merciful. His case presents us with a wonderful instance of what the gospel can do to soften the savage nature and bring even the most stubborn heart into sweet and willing subjection to our dear Redeemer. He was made a preacher of the gospel which had performed such wonders on his heart, and to the day of his death continued a faithful and devoted minister of the Lord Jesus.

While at Tavoy, a second child was born to this missionary family. They called him George, for his father. He yet lives — perhaps to bear the gospel forth to those who swarm around his father's grave.

At Tavoy, too, little Sarah died, when nearly

three years old. This child, the first born, seems to have twined its affections sweetly and tenderly around the mother's heart. She was indeed a lovely child. "Her bright-blue eyes and rosy cheeks," her amiable disposition and obedient deportment, won the kindness of all around her. She inherited the warm heart of her missionary mother, and fond hopes were cherished that she might live to fill her mother's place on heathen ground. But God's ways are not as our ways. He removed the lovely flower, and blasted in an hour all the fond expectations of her parents. In his infinite wisdom he saw the hinderance the little one would be to his laboring servant, and in kindness took her to his own arms.

When children die in this loved land they depart in the midst of tears and sighs; kind friends sympathize and pray; the voice of sorrow is heard along the line of many dwellings; and in many families is uttered the voice of grief. At such times and under such circumstances the hand of friendship and benevolence will be stretched out to assist and perform the little acts of charity which at such an hour come with sweet fragrance to the parting and weary spirit. But when little Sarah closed her eyes in death but few tears were seen, but few hands of sympathy held out. The broken-hearted mother herself washed the cold form of the dead child and arrayed the pale body in its little shroud.

On the mind of Mrs. Boardman this affliction

exerted a most salutary influence. She had admired and adored her child. She loved the precious gift more than the gracious Being who had bestowed it, and, wrapped up in its possession, imagined it could not be taken from her arms. But when God removed the loved and lovely one she began to feel how deeply she had erred, and forthwith restored her supreme affection to the great Creator. Her attention was called from the vain and transitory things of earth; she saw the narrow limit of human life more plainly than ever; she learned the lessons of mortality; and her sad bereavement became to her torn heart an inestimable blessing. Besides this, the idea that their little family had a representative in heaven was unutterably precious; and she feared less that hour when her own labors would be done and that reward entered upon which is prepared for all who obey God and love his Son Jesus Christ.

To Mrs. Boardman another child was also given, which was called Judson Wade Boardman — a trio of as illustrious names as ever were engraved on the records of the church militant. He lived but a short time, descending to the grave leaving another vacant place in the mother's heart.

In 1828 Mr. Boardman determined to leave Tavoy for a while and visit the Karen villages in the interior. He was accompanied by Ko Thah-byu and some other converted Karens. They had heard of him by means of persons who had visited Tavoy for business and pleasure, and religious books and tracts had been distributed among the people who had never heard a sermon or seen the pale face of the missionary. As he passed through their villages he was every where met with kindness. Food was brought and many valuable presents given him. At one village they found a zayat which the people had put up for them; and here they tarried and preached and explained the gospel several days. Many were converted; God's Spirit was poured out; and ere Mr. B. left the place several came and requested the ordinance of baptism. This matter, however, was prudently deferred, that the converts might "learn the way of the Lord more perfectly." He found the people in gross darkness: he left them with beams of light from the cross strong upon them. He found them without the word of God — without the Sabbath — without the way of salvation: he left them in the possession of all these good gifts, and at the end of nine days returned to his family at Tavoy, again to labor and suffer in the cause of his Master.

One of the most exciting incidents which occurred at Tavoy during the stay of Mr. B. was a rebellion, which commenced on the 9th of August, 1829. The English had withdrawn most of their soldiers from Tavoy and quartered them at Maulmain. Almost the whole force at the former place consisted of a hundred Sepoys, commanded by a man who, at the moment of the revolt, was believed to be in the agonies of death. On the 9th, at midnight, the missionary family were aroused by horrid cries around their rude dwelling. Boardman sprang from his bed, and, bending his ear to the open window, heard the cry, " Teacher, Tavoy is in arms! Tavoy is in arms!" In an instant the ready mind of the missionary comprehended the difficulty and the danger. He at once aroused his family, and began to prepare for resistance or flight as the case might require. After a time the insurgents were repulsed, and, retiring to a distance, took refuge in rear of the mission buildings; consequently the station was placed between the two contending parties; and over the heads of the little band the balls whistled, carrying death to hated foes. In the morning the Sepoys were driven from the city and took refuge in the Government House, to which place the missionary family repaired, seizing for this a momentary quiet. Their situation here was terrible. The house was crowded with women and children . soon it became unsafe, and the whole party retired to a vacant building, having six rooms, on the margin of the river. Into this house, containing more than a hundred barrels of powder, were three hundred persons crowded together; while without were heard the wild and frantic yells of the savages, thirsting for blood. On the morning of the 13th

Mr. Burney, the civil superintendent, who was away at the time of the outbreak, returned. To him the whole people were indebted for their safety and their lives. Under his management the Sepoys rallied and advanced upon the city, and, after several desperate conflicts, succeeded in driving the insurgents from it and capturing several of the leaders in the revolt. The overwhelming number of the foe was not proof against the superior skill of the English; and when the vessel which had been sent to Maulmain for help returned, Major Burney was in quiet possession of the town.

Mrs. Boardman immediately embarked for Maulmain; to which place her husband soon followed her, taking with him all the scholars in the school who were willing to go. They remained at M. until the mission house was repaired and quiet restored.

From this period up to the time of her husband's last sickness we find but little in the history of Mrs. Boardman of a marked character. She labored on under discouragements and difficulties and amid sickness and sorrow. Often did her own system give way; and more often did her child utter the wail of sickness and distress, and plead for rest and quiet which could not be granted. During this interval Mr. B. made repeated journeys from Tavoy to Maulmain, and was busily engaged in the great object of his life. He saw to some extent the fruits of his toil; and on his abundant labors Heaven placed the broad seal of divine approbation. One after another yielded to the force of truth and bowed in homage to the cross of Christ. He did not die, like Coleman and Wheelock, ere he had seen the heathen eye overflow with tears, the heathen heart burst with rapture into life, and the heathen knees bowing, not before Gaudama, but before Jehovah.

During the year 1830 it became evident to all that Mr. Boardman must die. The disease contracted in consequence of sleeping on the cold ground and being exposed to the damp fogs of night came on slowly but surely, and all hope of recovery took its flight. Feeling himself that he should soon depart, he called the converts around him and instructed them in the way of life. Others who had not been baptized he prepared for the ordinance. Three days were devoted to the examination, and eighteen were accepted as candidates for the holy service. The missionary was unable to rise from his bed; and many of the questions which he desired to put to these persons were first given to his wife, who, sitting on the bed beside him, put her ear to his lips and caught the sound as it struggled for utterance. On the 20th of December the baptism took place under circumstances of thrilling interest. The candidates, with the administrator, and the sick teacher, borne on a little cot upon the shoulders of the Karens, passed along to a fine lake, into which Moung Ing descended and immersed the young disciples. It was a sight of interest to God and angels; and doubtless they bent over the scene with holy satisfaction. As they went to the place and as they returned the wicked idolaters jeered and scoffed, and heaped their maledictions upon the head of the dying Boardman, who in a short time was to be far beyond the reach of injury and insult.

The administration of the Lord's supper followed the baptismal service, to which the little church of twenty-seven members sat down, eighteen of them for the first time. The bread was broken by the trembling, dying hand of Mr. Boardman, who was performing the deed for *the last* time.

In January, 1831, Mr. and Mrs. Mason arrived at Tavoy, having been sent out to reënforce the mission, and were immediately conducted to the residence of their dying fellow-laborer. The meeting of the two devoted men and their wives must have been of deep and solemn interest. One was fresh from the land of his birth, ready to engage with zeal in the Master's work; the other had fought the fight, had kept the faith, had finished the course, and was about to receive the robe of victory and the crown of glory.

Wishing to make one more effort in the cause of his Savior, Mr. Boardman determined to visit the village where a short time before he had preached several days and where several persons had been converted. These he wished to gather into the fold, and, ere his departure, see them buried in the liquid grave. He went forth with his newly-arrived associates and his own family. A company of Karens carried Mr. Boardman on a bed and Mrs. B. in a chair. After a journey of three days they arrived at the place and found the villagers in anxious expectation. They had erected a church on the banks of a lovely stream and prepared accommodations for the missionaries. After the converts had been properly instructed, they were baptized by Mr. Mason. Thirty-four submitted to the ordinance and were added to the little band of believers. The journey and the effort made to commune with the people were too much for the exhausted frame, and the good man began to sink rapidly. Carefully they took him up to remove him to the boat which was to convey him to the river; but as they passed along, the anxious wife, who watched the countenance of her husband, saw a change. Death had stamped his signet on those pale features; and, when they arrived at the water side, all that remained of Boardman was a cold, inanimate corpse. The voyage down the river was a sorrowful one. Every check was flowing down with tears and every heart was bleeding with anguish.

At Tavoy they were met by the sad disciples

headed by Moung Ing, the converted Burman. Slowly they bore forward the dead body of the man of God, and laid it down in the mission house in which he had so often discoursed of Jesus. Around him in that hallowed spot gathered a company more precious to God than ever assembled around the bier of a fallen emperor; there went up to heaven a wail of sorrow as heartfelt as ever was uttered over the grave of son or sire; and the death was as full of sadness and importance as could have been the demise of a laurelled chieftain or a titled senator. True, the throng who came out to see that pale form and marble brow were not gathered from the proud and great of earth. No king came weeping to the house of death; no noble *cortége* came in sackcloth and stood as mourners there; but the elect of God, the fruits of missionary labor on heathen soil, the converted sons and daughters of darkness, were the sincere, humble, faithful mourners.

They buried him in lowly pomp — *the pomp of death.* All the European residents of the place and crowds of natives to whom he had endeared himself followed him to his burial. They laid him down on the right side of his first born, and returned home to weep, and many to *forget*. But there was one who could never forget — no, never. The object of her early love had been stricken down, and in lonely widowhood she was left to bewail his loss.

But, though cast down, she was not forsaken. The Savior was her portion; and in this hour of trial she leaned on him. In her terrible visitation she saw the traces of Jehovah's care; and, committing herself and her fatherless child to him, her soul rested in hope.

During the time which elapsed between the death of Mr. Boardman and her marriage with Dr. Judson the afflicted widow labored with all her might to do the will of her Master. Not content with instructing the lisping child and tender youth, she travelled from village to village with her little boy and a few attendants. Wherever she went she was met with kindness. The death of the white teacher had unsealed even the wild heart of heathenism; and the widow was an object of universal interest. It is doubtful if at any period of her life she exhibited more lovely traits of character, or accomplished a greater amount of good in an equal space of time, than while moving along her tearful way from the grave of one husband to the marriage chamber of another.

After having remained a widow four years, Mrs. B. was, in April, 1834, united in marriage to Dr. Judson The parties were well acquainted with each other, and both understood the wants and privations of a missionary life. This new marriage was a new proof of devotion to Christ and his cause; and when Mrs. B. a second time gave herself to a missionary husband, it was a new and sublime token of her determination to live a missionary life. Had she been so disposed, she might have returned to the home and friends of her youth; but, with a full conception of all that would await her, she again gave herself, for. life, to Jesus and the perishing heathen.

Her little George, who had been to her torn and lacerated heart such a source of comfort, began to fail; and his mother determined to send him to America. But how could she part with her darling one? How could she behold him borne away to a distant land, to see her face no more? But with the same submission which she had ever manifested she bowed to this new bereavement, and kissed the cheek of her child and sent him away. It was a trial for which she had prepared herself; and it proved almost equal to any which had preceded it. But, knowing the importance of the step, she cheerfully acquiesced with the fortitude of a Christian.

It was not alone on heathen minds that Mrs. Judson produced a pleasant influence. The English residents at Tavoy, Maulmain, and Calcutta remember her with affectionate interest. Many of them have in their houses or about their persons the tokens of her kindness; and not a few can look back to hours of sickness and affliction when a gentle hand smoothed the pillow and a kind voice whispered in the ear words of hope and heaven. Often did she meet in the praying circle with those who, like her, were far from home, and exhort them to love and serve God; and in obedience to her kind instructions many sought and found the Savior. For a prayer meeting of mothers she wrote a beautiful hymn, which appeared in a journal in our country, which is truly touching and beautiful. It is as follows: —

" Lamb of God, enthroned on high,
Look on us with pitying eye
While we raise our earnest cry
  For our babes to thee.

Once thy followers infants spurned;
But thy bosom o'er them yearned,
Nor from Canaan's daughters turned
  Thy all-pitying eye.

Thou didst give *our* spirits rest,
When with sin and grief oppressed,
In thy gentle, loving breast:
  Shelter, then, our babes.

Breath divine they breathe, and **wear**
God's own image; yet they bear
Sin and guilt a fearful share:
  Pity them, we pray.

Guide and guard them here below,
As through dangerous paths they go;
Be their joy 'mid earthly woe —
  Thou, their heavenly Friend.

> When, to call thy children home,
> Robed in glory thou shalt come,
> For these little ones make room,
> Lamb of God, we pray."

Her union with Dr. Judson was a happy one Four little babes were born unto them ere the mother was called to try the realities of that world where there are no separations. In the care and culture of these much of her time was necessarily spent; and so excessive and fatiguing were her labors that she soon began to sink under them. After the birth of her last child, which was born in December, 1844, it became evident to her husband that he was soon to be left alone. The wasting disease made its appearance, and the pale form bowed beneath it. Her kind and experienced physicians, as a last resort, recommended a voyage to America; and, after much consideration and prayer, she determined to turn her back on Burmah and once more visit the land of her nativity. A passage to this country was immediately secured; and, in company with her husband, she set sail in the early part of 1845. They had no sooner embarked than her health began to amend; and when they reached the Isle of France Dr. Judson determined to return to his labors, and leave his companion to visit America alone. They made their arrangements to part — the one to labor and faint, the other to greet kind friends in an often-remembered land. On the Isle of France the beautiful poem, commencing, —

"We part on this green islet, love,"—

was written — a poem as affecting and heart-touching, when the circumstances are recounted, as any one ever written.

But, on putting out to sea again, the disease returned with new symptoms of alarm, and continued to increase until September 1, 1845, when she died within sight of the rocky Island of St. Helena.

Thus a second time was the venerable Judson bereaved of his dear companion, and in the midst of strangers called upon to surrender up the remains of the loved one to corruption and decay. They buried her where the hero of Lodi and Austerlitz slept, and a long train of mourners followed her to the tomb. The flags of the vessels in the harbor were seen waving at half mast, and signs of woe were observed in all directions.

She died in holy triumph, feeling that her labors were done, her toils finished, her race ended, and her warfare accomplished. To the husband who sat beside her when her last breath was drawn she said, just before she expired, "I ever love the Lord Jesus;" and with her hand in his, her soul leaning for support on the almighty arm, she sunk to rest. The sight which St. Helena saw that day was a sad one — more sad than when the leader of the defeated armies of France was laid to rest beneath its soil.

Perhaps this sketch of Mrs. J. cannot be brought to a close more appropriately than by the introduction of a beautiful extract from an address made by a distinguished statesman of New England at a missionary convention in Philadelphia — an address which contains a beautiful reference to the fallen missionary, to the labors of those who are now on heathen soil, and to the sufferings of our Lord Jesus Christ while on earth performing his labor of love and fulfilling his mission of grace to fallen man. —

"It is undoubtedly true that you are sometimes called upon to make sacrifices in your work of love. You sometimes feel that you are making sacrifices. It may be comparatively so; but really, if you look at it as it is, you will find it no very great sacrifice. Here are our brethren who have left their homes and friends, who have gone among strangers and heathens. We have heard the story of their deprivations, of their labors, of their sorrows, of their chains, and of their imprisonment. Many of them mourn over departed happiness; many of them have fallen in the great work, and now sleep in heathen lands; many of them have gone down to the bottom of the great deep, where the seaweed is their winding sheet, the coral their only tombstone. One sleeps in Helena till the sound of the last trumpet arouse her; and when she comes up she will be attended by a retinue ten thousand times more pompous and more splendid than ever surrounded the maddened emperor who had his grave in that island. His tomb was there, and after a few years, when it was opened, his military dress was wrapped around him as when he was laid there; but the star upon his bosom, the emblem of his glory, the pride of his life, — it was corroded and black, a true representation of human glory, of the glory of a conqueror and an imperial murderer. But when the grave shall open, and that loved sister Judson shall come forth, there will be no corroded stars over that heart. But those who are there, as I said before, have certainly made sacrifices compared with us, with the brethren and friends they left behind; but when they look in another direction, when they turn their eyes to the great field, they feel fully compensated. They may live upon rice and milk, and often not have enough of that. Their frail tenements are broken down by the storms; and they are exposed to the roaming tigers, who may spring upon and rush through the thin walls of their habitations. They may be imprisoned for a while and racked by the chains of tyranny. Yet never have they been compelled to exclaim, as did that Savior who came to his own and his own received him not, when a Pharisee proposed to be his follower, 'The birds of the air have nests and the foxes have holes; but the

Son of man hath not where to lay his head.' Think of that, ye heralds of the cross, — think of that. brethren in foreign lands, — the Being who made the world, while here in the flesh, declaring that the birds which he had made had nests, and the foxes he had created had holes, where they could rest and sleep in security, but no place on this earth he had made where he could quietly lay that majestic, godlike head! Sometimes you feel as though your friends had forsaken you. Go to Gethsemane; see there that Master who but a short time before, with the twelve surrounding the table, had told them of the approaching trials and dangers: urged to rashness, the unthinking Peter had declared that, although all others might forsake him, he would not. He goes into that lonely garden, separating himself from his disciples; but he takes Peter, with two others, and asks them to watch here a while, while he goes yonder and prays. And then that traitor Judas had gone to make his bargain; and the Savior knew the bands were hunting him. O think of that hour and that garden! Think of the agony of that Savior's heart, which made him say, 'My heart is exceeding sorrowful, even unto death'! Think of the agony, when the blood from the pores of his skin dropped down on Gethsemane's garden, and when he came up to the judgment hall the noisy rabble insulting him; his followers abandoning him; the man who two short hours before had said to him, 'that though all others forsake thee, I will not,' uttering curses in his hearing and denying that he ever knew him; then the scarlet robe and that crown of thorns! O, has earth ever witnessed such a spectacle as that? And then that cowardly Roman governor, though he knew he was innocent, yielded him up to the hands of a vociferous, noisy, and infuriated mob; and he was by him condemned to an ignominious death. In the service of such a Master, who of his followers would talk of sacrifice? And then the consummation upon the cross, when all the powers of darkness on earth and hell were defeated! Three days, and on the morning of the first day of the week that buffeted, that down-trodden, and crucified Savior burst the shackles of the tomb, laid the monster Death at his feet, and rose a triumphant conqueror over the grave."

CHAPTER X.

ANNIE P. JAMES,

OF CHINA.

*I*N the beautiful city of Salem Mrs. Annie P. James was born, on the 22d of December, 1825. She was the beloved daughter of Joshua and Sarah Safford, old and much-esteemed residents of that place. She was reared not far from the spot where young Sarah Hall caught the fire of missionary devotion and consecrated herself to the work of Heaven. Her childhood was passed in the very centre of missionary feeling and action: in a city where the hallowed influence of Worcester and Bolles will long be felt, though those venerated men have descended to the grave; in a city where the first consecration was made, and Judson and his associates set apart to missionary life.

The early years of Mrs. James were spent in the home of her parents, who made every suitable exertion to develop the powers of her mind and cultivate the moral faculties. Under their influence she grew up to womanhood distinguished for her amiable disposition, pure heart, and vigorous intellect. By a large circle of associates she was much beloved; and when the intelligence of her death came, she was most seriously mourned.

When less than ten years of age she commenced a journal, which was continued more or less regularly to the time of her death. Even at that early age she evinced profound thought, and many of the entries made exhibit evidences of much maturity of mind. Her School Journal and the essays read to her teacher were far beyond her years, and excited the admiration of those to whom the care of her instruction had been committed. Her Text Book, in which she weekly recorded the services of the sanctuary, is filled with plans of sermons, very correctly reported and very neatly written.

As she advanced in life, Annie gave new evidences of an active mind and a lovely disposition. Friends increased, and her society was sought by many who loved her for her virtues and respected her for her intellect.

In 1842 her heart was changed, and she became a child of God. To an amiable disposition were added a regenerated soul and a blood-washed conscience. Christ was formed within her, the hope of glory; and from henceforth he was her life. Her own record of her Christian experience is as follows:—

"As far as I can remember, it has been my intention from a child to become a Christian. I knew that I must not *die* without being one; so I used to pray that my death might be that of the righteous. My conscience was a very faithful monitor; but I neglected all its warnings, and would heed none of its reproofs. Still I prayed daily to my heavenly Father that he would bless me. At times I felt almost persuaded to be a Christian, and yet would silence my conscience by resolving to be good, and yet serve the world — serve God and Mammon also.

"But soon my heart began to grow harder. I plunged deeply into the world's pleasures; I almost forgot my God. Gradually my evening prayer was omitted, and I only prayed in the hour of danger Still my Father did not forsake me; but when I cried he heard and answered me, and all was peace again.

"I continued thus until Rev. Mr. Anderson came to the city. I went to hear him, and became deeply interested in his discourses. Aware that I must delay no longer, — that now, and perhaps now *only*, was the accepted time, — I felt that my condemnation must be great indeed, because I had known my duty and had not performed it.

"I attended the inquiry meetings. This I felt to be taking a decided stand, and determined never to go back. My pastor told me to give my heart unreservedly to God and believe on the Savior; but my stubborn will still held out. I had not *fully* resolved; but through the mercy of my heavenly Father I finally yielded; and I now trust I have found peace in believing."

From the time of her conversion she gave delightful evidence of a renewed mind and heart, and shed around the holy influence of the Christian life. So impressed was the church with the change that she was invited to unite herself with the people of God; and accordingly, on the 19th of August, was examined as a candidate for membership.

She was publicly baptized on the first Sabbath in September. Rev. Mr. Anderson, with whose church she united, led her down into the consecrated wave, and in the presence of a vast assembly her public vows were performed. The same day she received the "right hand of fellowship;" and as the Sabbath closed, and the sun went down in loveliness behind the western hills, she took her seat at the communion table to enjoy for the first time the dear and precious services of the holy sacrament. Her connection with the church opened to her new fields of usefulness. She became deeply interested in home and foreign missions, and, up to the time of her leaving home, did much to inspire her young fellow-disciples with a true missionary spirit. She was elected corresponding secretary of the Boardman Missionary Society — an organization constituted for missionary purposes. While holding this office she presented to the body several interesting reports, which are full of information in reference to our western Indians and other destitute tribes of men. One of her letters written while performing her duties as secretary, directed to Rev. Willard P. Upham, who is laboring among the Cherokee Indians, will be read with interest : —

"SALEM, May 12, 1845.

"RESPECTED BROTHER, — Yours of the 9th was received; and I can truly say we were much interested in its contents. A special meeting was called at the vestry for its perusal, as we thought the request to the church should be immediately attended to; after this it was sent to your own family and to that of our pastor.

"Your description of the baptism of our brethren of the forest was so touching, and the scene so faithfully delineated, that we could almost imagine ourselves eye witnesses of it all. Surely there must be unwonted joy in the courts of heaven when the angels, as they gaze on earth, behold the savage himself subdued beneath the power of Prince Immanuel, and in Nature's own temple worshipping his and 'Nature's God.' And how great, too, must be your happiness in being personally interested in this glorious change!

"That such joy may be often yours is our most

sincere wish; and therefore we cordially comply with your request, and send this dress, (a baptismal robe,) hoping you will be called to wear it very frequently in your Master's service; and as it reminds you of those whom you once called your friends, may your prayers ascend in their behalf, bringing down blessings upon them."

But these labors were soon to be exchanged for more arduous and responsible ones; and the youthful servant of Christ was to go forth from home, from friends, from happy circles, to find *a watery grave*, a resting-place, beneath the bosom of the wave. In the early part of 1847 Dr. Sexton James visited Salem, and tarried a few days at the residence of a former classmate. During his visit he became acquainted with Miss Safford. A resemblance between her and his former deceased wife first drew his attention; and very soon her amiable disposition, refined and cultivated manners, educated mind, and ardent piety won his affections and enlisted all his feelings. He met with her abroad, in the place of prayer, in social gatherings, and at her own home; and the intimacy resulted in a proposal of marriage and a missionary life. Her parents at first opposed the union. They could not endure the idea of sending out their darling child to distant China. The sacrifice was too great, the treasure of too much value, to lay upon the altar of God. They were both warmhearted Christians; but the service of Christ had never called upon them for *such* a sacrifice before; and it is not strange that they should shrink back.

The mind of the daughter was perplexed. She heard the call of duty, but would not obey while her parents were so unreconciled. The day after her decision was made she penned a letter to her beloved pastor, Rev. Thomas D. Anderson, who was then in Washington, being in feeble health. The letter, an extract from which we give, is under date of May 14, 1847. After speaking of the proposal of Dr. James, she says, "Father said, decidedly, he could not consent. My mother was agonized at the idea of a separation; and she, too, felt that she could not let me go, although she was not prepared to say I should not. Sarah (her sister) was almost frantic with grief; and you can imagine how I must have felt. From long conversation with Dr. James, I became convinced it was my duty to go, if the loved ones here could be brought to feel that it really was so and give a willing consent; otherwise I would not go — *I could not.* Thus the matter remained undecided. We made it a subject of prayer, and left the result with God, knowing 'he doeth all things well;' and if we could only say, 'Thy will be done,' it was all he required.

"God has changed the feelings of my parents;

they 'cannot fight' against his almighty will; and there are so many rich mercies mingled in the cup of sorrow that they have resolved to drink it, and trust in him for strength and support in all that he may require. They have given me to my Savior; and now the path of duty appears plain to us all."

The manner in which this change in the minds of her parents was brought about is somewhat singular. At the request of Dr. James, they set apart one day — a holy Sabbath — to pray for guidance in reference to this matter. On that Sabbath morning they arose from a sleepless pillow, resolved to keep their child and deny the claims of Jesus; but ere the sun went down in beauty behind the hills they had re-resolved, and on the altar of divine obedience had consecrated themselves and their daughter. Previous to this change of feeling Annie was in doubt as to the path of duty; and a letter which she wrote to Dr. J. about one month previous presents her in a most beautiful light. She says to him as follows: —

"I have thought could I only talk with you by pen and paper, rather than 'face to face,' perhaps I should find it far easier to express my feelings on this momentous subject; but now that I have really undertaken to do so, it still appears very difficult May God direct me in this duty!

"The longer I have thought upon the result of my determination in this matter, the more powerful it seems. Clouds and darkness are round about it; and so dense are they, I am afraid I cannot see duty through them. Unless the way is clear, I surely ought not to go; and to me it does not appear so. I find myself bound by the strongest ties to my country and my home. My absence renders miserable those I love dearest, and to whom, next my God, I am under the strongest obligations. They have watched over me from infancy, spending the best portion of their lives in efforts for my good, and with self-sacrificing devotion sought my happiness, and in this found their own. Now that the burden of years rests upon them, and the strength with which they have labored is well nigh exhausted, and they look to me to repay their unwearied devotion, *can I forsake them*, can I burst the ties which unite us to each other, and which are so interwoven about our hearts that they have become, as it were, parts of our very nature? Can I sever these and leave them? It seems to me no earthly affection should induce me so to do.

"If I am what I profess to be, I am not my own. 'I am bought with a price,' and hence belong to Him who hath redeemed me. At his call I should be willing to say, 'Here, Lord, I am; do with me as seemeth good in thy sight;' and 'not my will, but thine, be done.' In this view of the matter, it follows that I ought to be very certain what God *does* really require of me. I have not been deeply impressed that it is my duty to leave those whom he hath told me to 'honor and obey' for a home beyond the ocean, where the people sit in the region and shadow of death. I have not been sufficiently urged by a sense of duty in this. I have not sufficiently felt the force of the command, 'Go teach;' but I fear I have simply had my affections enlisted for one who possesses traits of character such as I have always been accustomed to love. Wherever and whenever I meet 'a spirit that can answer mine,' I love it. Therefore, although I feel that I should deeply prize a heart like yours, and should be most happy to call it mine, yet this should not be my motive to action. Here I must leave it; for I am not prepared to go further. I still think it will be decidedly best for you to return to your home ere I make a final decision. I ought not, and must not, let you acquire such an influence over my mind as to induce me to rush on with mistaken zeal in a path my God has not marked out for me.

"With our God let us leave the matter. May he direct us aright, and cause all things to work together for our good.

ANNIE."

This letter, designed for one reader only, shows the contest in the young mind between duty to God and the heathen, and what she seemed to feel was duty to her loved parents; and nobly does it speak for the youthful writer.

After the change in the minds of her parents, her own duty was soon decided. She resolved to leave father and mother, and go out with Dr. J. to his distant field of labor. Anxious to know to what conclusion she had arrived, and what he was to expect, he went to her for the final decision. After a few minutes spent in conversation, she placed a note in his hands, informing him that it contained her determination upon the subject, and requested him not to open it until he arrived at his residence. The temptation to open the letter was too strong; the contents were too intimately connected with his usefulness; too much depended on the decision which she had made to allow the last injunction to remain long heeded. When a few rods from the house, crossing Washington Square, he took the document, expecting to find a long epistle, filled with reasons, explanations, plans, &c.; but what was his surprise and admiration to find these lines only: "Whither thou goest I will go; and where thou lodgest I will lodge; thy people shall be my people, and thy God my God; where thou diest will I die, and there will I be buried"! Had she known the manner of her death, she could not have penned a sentence more sweet, more touching, more appropriate.

On the 15th day of June Dr. James and Miss Safford were married in the First Baptist Church in Salem by Rev. Thomas D. Anderson. A few weeks were spent in travel, during which time the bride visited for the first time the friends of her husband in Philadelphia. In that city the farewell service was held, a description of which is given in a letter from Dr. Wilson Jewell, who was an intimate friend of Dr. James. This letter, though written only for the inspection of the parents, we are permitted to make public: —

"Philadelphia, November 1, 1847.

"My dear Friends. — Feeling a deep interest in all the scenes connected with the departure of my young friends. Dr. Sexton James and his amiable companion, as missionaries to China, and knowing full well your parental anxiety and the peculiar emotions which swell your bosoms at this eventful crisis, the agonizing period through which you have just passed, the overwhelming trial you have been called in the providence of God to endure, and for which nothing but the grace of God has prepared you, — in giving up a dear child, a daughter too, perhaps for life, together with her expected embarkation in a few days for the far-off land of China, — I esteem it a privilege, as some remuneration for the kindness shown me during the few hours I sojourned at your hospitable mansion, and as some little consolation in the midst of your sorrow, to communicate to you of the precious farewell missionary meeting held this evening in the Tenth Church, where your dear child and her excellent husband were the objects of fervent prayer and anxious solicitude. A more solemn, more interesting, more heart-moving meeting I never attended before. The house was crowded. The Baptist churches in the city generally gave up the monthly concert, and many of their members attended. Nine of our city pastors and eight other ministering brethren were present on the occasion. The Rev. Mr. Kingsford, after one of the most appropriate and beautiful addresses, gave the right hand of fellowship, on behalf of the Board of Missions, to Brother James and Annie: they both stood up in the front pew where they had been seated; Mr. K. descended from the desk and took their hands. O that you could have been present and have beheld the modest firmness and the Christian dignity of your loved child! Then came Sexton's classmate and friend, the Rev. Heman Lincoln, Jr., who addressed him in the sweetest language I ever listened to. It was a most tender and heart-melting speech. He alluded to by-gone college scenes, their conversion, the little praying circle in which they had often met, their prayers for each other, and their college companions. He spoke of those who had gone from earth to heavenly joys, and of those who were left, one of whom (Rev. Thomas Malcom,) besides himself, was present. There was not a heart which did not feel and throb with tender emotions. The mournful sob and the half-suppressed sigh could be heard all over the house. I never was in such a meeting before. I never beheld such sorrow and joy mingled together. Brother Malcom followed brother Lincoln in prayer, made suitable for the passing scene. Next came Sexton's pastor, Rev. Joseph H. Kennard, who, in one of his pathetic and affectionate addresses, presented a small pocket Bible to him, and then gave him and Annie the parting hand on behalf of the church. This was most affecting of all: the gushing tears and the loud sobs were again seen and heard. In the midst of this most interesting service, Mr. I. E. James, the father of Sexton, rose up and interrupted the speaker just at the point where he was alluding to the struggle of mind which it had cost the parent to part with the child, and said, 'I feel it due to myself to say this evening, that, although it has cost me many a painful struggle, I can give them up for Christ's sake;' and, turning his face towards Sexton and Annie, said, with emphasis, 'I give you up for Christ's sake.' This was too much for the strongest nerves. The effect was overwhelming; the scene was indescribable.

"During the evening exercises, a number of pastors led in prayer and several appropriate chapters of the Bible were read. The most fervent petitions were made for our dear young friends, and every Christian heart present said 'Amen.' It was a meeting long to be remembered; a meeting of power, of the presence of God's Spirit, and one not only of fervent but I trust of effectual prayer. I would that you had been there; it was indeed a heavenly place in Christ Jesus. Sexton and your dear Annie bore up well under the trial. God supported them by faith; they seemed to lean on his holy word; and I doubt not the same like precious faith will be ministered to them in all their future journey by flood or field. God's promises are yea and amen in Christ.

"We are all very much endeared to Annie, and every day she is with us she gains new friends: it is only to see her to love her. We regret the time is so short; but shall *we* not give her up also? O, how I envy that parent's faith who can give away a child for Christ's sake, and such a child!"

The vessel which bore them out was the good ship Valparaiso; and we will allow Mrs. James to give her own account of the embarkation and the voyage:—

"November 11, 1847.

"A bright sun and a cloudless sky told us the day had really come for our departure. We partook of an early dinner in sadness, and then all knelt together for worship. Sexton prayed, and father followed; and then came the parting service, and we were gone. Our carriage arrived at the wharf after the religious services were concluded and the vessel cast off. We therefore took a boat and went out, after giving and receiving the farewell kiss from many who gathered around us. We are surrounded, not only with the comforts, but with the luxuries of life. Our room is a sweet place, commodious and beautifully furnished."

"DELAWARE RIVER, November 13, 1847.

"DEAR PARENTS,—We are still at anchor opposite Newcastle, and shall probably remain here till Monday. While they were weighing anchor, very early this morning, to proceed to sea, some of the castings connected with the windlass were broken, and have to be repaired.

"Our delay has been very pleasant, as we are able to put every thing to rights and feel ourselves at home before proceeding to sea. We already feel so, and are very happy. We certainly have every thing to make us so. We have most delightful accommodations; our cabin to-night looks as rich and cheerful as any parlor; a good lamp not only casts a flood of light around, but warms our room, although it is cold without. We have just had evening worship — singing, reading, and prayer

Your son Sexton read two psalms and prayed. We have had a delightful season. Our fellow-passengers are exceedingly pleasant, and we expect to enjoy their company very much. We have been taking exercise to-day on deck."

"SABBATH EVENING, November 14, 1847.

"MY DEAR ONES, — The Sabbath has passed away quietly with us. You will see, by the addition I have made to Sexton's letter, that he has not felt very well to-day. He has had a slight attack of inflammation. But, by the blessing of God and the use of means, we have, I trust, arrested the disease. He is very nicely this evening; no pain, and but little soreness. The whole has been very slight. He has been his own physician, and I his nurse.

"The captain returned early this afternoon, and, all things being in readiness, we weighed anchor and glided down, at the rate of eight knots an hour, to this place, (about thirty miles below Newcastle.) We have scarcely realized the motion of the vessel, although she sailed so rapidly. The captain is much pleased with her manner of sailing, and appears quite happy to-night. He came into our room and made us a social call this evening. He is all kindness to us. We have every thing to make us happy. I cannot realize I am on shipboard, all is so beautiful about me."

The following letter is from Dr. James: —

"SHIP VALPARAISO, November 22, 1847.

"DEAR PARENTS, — Sail ho! from the mast head. Joyful cry! As we may possibly 'speak' her, I will have a few lines in readiness. We have had a most prosperous voyage thus far. We left the line of the Cape of Delaware Bay on Monday noon. Annie was handled pretty severely by seasickness for two days, but since then she has been sick but little. She is still weak, but I think will regain her strength in a few days. I feel grateful that she has not suffered more. I have been sick only about three minutes, since which time I have been able to attend to Annie's wants. I have taken her upon deck about every day, where she has remained lying upon a settee from morn till night. It has been of great service to her. I am in hopes she will not be sick again.

"The Valparaiso is a very dry ship: although we sailed fast, we have not had a sprinkling upon deck. We have much to be grateful for, and I trust are not unmindful of the Source from whence these blessings flow. That 'same smile' continues to attend us, and I trust always may, however dark the face of man around may be.

"I wish you were here to take tea and spend the evening with us; though I am afraid the motions of the ship would incommode you *landsmen* a little.

Next Thursday will be Thanksgiving day. You must reserve plates for us, for we shall be with you — in spirit."

The next letter given is from Mrs. James: —

"December 18, 1847.

"My dear Parents, — This is a delightful summer morning, though in the middle of December. We have our windows open, and are enjoying the full benefit of the sea breeze. I am much better; breakfasted well this morning, and have for my lunch a nice flying fish, which came on deck this morning — a kind of food which is said to be delicious. Sexton has cut off his wings and is drying them. From my window the other day I saw a whole school of them darting out of the midst of the waves. One day, while on deck, I saw a large whale bounding through the deep waters. Our company have also seen porpoises and dolphins playing around. One evening the captain invited us on deck to see the phosphorescence by which we were surrounded. It was a scene well worth gazing upon. Clouds of it burst from the bosom of the wave and rendered it all brightness. They that go down to the sea in ships see the wonders of the Lord in the mighty deep.

"Last Sabbath I went to meeting and heard a sermon from Mr. Baldwin. His text was that beautiful passage from the Psalms, 'O that men would praise the Lord for his goodness and his wonderful works unto the children of men!' It was a most interesting spectacle to see the rough seamen, neatly attired, listening to the words which fell from the preacher's lips. The voice of prayer and the song of praise were sweet indeed."

"December 27, 1847.

"Yesterday we had a delightful Sabbath: our time passes pleasantly away. I cannot realize that I have been on the ocean so long, or that I am more than six thousand miles from my dearly-loved home. In dreams I often visit you, and see the old friends long since departed, who look so natural.

"Sexton is in excellent health, and weighs one hundred and twenty-one pounds; while his poor wife does not quite reach one hundred and one."

"SHIP VALPARAISO, January 9, 1848.

"MY DEAR SISTER, — I thought this pleasant Sabbath afternoon I would talk a while with you. I do wish you could peep in upon us, to see how comfortably we are situated in our floating home. God has been very good to us, sister, and we are surrounded by many mercies.

"We attended public service on deck this morning, and heard a sermon preached by Mr. Cummings from the words, 'This is a faithful saying and worthy of all acceptation,' &c. It is very pleasant to see our hardy crew, neatly attired, and listening to truth which is able to make them wise unto salvation. I hope these seasons may not be wholly lost upon them, but that good may be done, and seed sown in their hearts which sooner or later will spring up to the glory of God.

"We held a female prayer meeting in my room this noon and had a very pleasant season. I let mother come,* and after meeting Mrs. C. kissed her. And then I looked at you all; but this made me sad; for when I see your dear, familiar faces, I think how much better a child I might have been, and how much better a sister I might have been, when I was with you: these thoughts trouble me. I cannot now atone for omissions of duty which memory brings to my view; but I will seek forgiveness from my God, who is merciful and gracious.

"February 10, 1848.

"Dear Sister, — I have just come from the female prayer meeting, where we have been asking God to bring *you* into the covenant of his grace. Our meeting was scarcely finished when we heard the joyful sound, 'Sail, ho!' We were soon on deck; and there, far off, we saw a white speck resting apparently against the sky. It grew upon us

---

* Reference to miniature portraits.

while we gazed, and with a glass we saw it to be indeed a vessel. O, how happy we felt! The captain told us he thought it bound for England; and says, if so, we shall send letters by her. Still it is all a matter of uncertainty; but we are writing as fast as we can.

"I have been on deck again, and find that the strange vessel is bearing down upon us; so I will add a few lines. We have the prospect of a long passage; so you must not feel anxious about us, and must not look for a letter until the last of July. We have been delayed by head winds and calms, so that we make but little progress. Yet this is no cause for fear. We have a fine sea boat, and every thing is going on well. We have had but comparatively few gales; and during these our noble ship bore herself gallantly, and our heavenly Father kept us from all harm. Time passes swiftly with us, although we see nothing but the ocean bounded by the sky. Not a speck of land has greeted our eyes since we left the shores of our own dear America. We hoped to have made some of the islands during our passage; but it was not so to be; and it is doubtless all for the best. We have been within eighty miles of New Holland. If we could only have a good breeze, we should make Sandalwood Islands in a few days; but now we have nearly a dead calm: the ocean is very still, and scarcely any motion is perceptible. The thermometer was at eighty-six over our breakfast table this morning; so you may be sure it is warm enough. We have glorious moonlight evenings, and we enjoy them We trace out stars and constellations, and sit or walk on the deck and talk of them. Last evening we noticed particularly your Pleiades: they looked like sparkling diamonds, they were so brilliant.

"February 11, 1848.

"Dear Uncle and Aunt, — We have had a quiet, pleasant day on the ocean, and can write as easily as if we were sitting in our parlors at home. Now, I suppose you would like to know what sort of a sailor I make and how I like my new situation. Well, I must confess I thought at first the sea was no place for ladies, and would have rejoiced to have been once more on land; but these days have passed now. I was very seasick, more so than any one you ever saw; but I had every thing done for me that kindness could do, and now I am well and happy.

"We have a beautiful room, with three large windows in it, the locker under them cushioned with velvet, and every thing comfortable and convenient around. The other half of the stern of our ship is furnished as a parlor; and we use it when we please. The state rooms are each side of the main cabin, and are occupied by the passengers, of which there are two gentlemen, with their wives, one single lady, one single gentleman, and a Chinese woman. Beyond these the captain and Charles have their rooms; and then comes the bath room, steward's pantry, and pastry room.

"God is very good to us. Every want is supplied, and he only asks us in return to love him and be thankful. It is strange that we are so unwilling to do our heavenly Father's will when he is so kind to us. We have now been out eighty-eight days, and are expecting a long passage, because we have been so detained by head winds and calms. The greatest run we have made in twenty-four hours has been two hundred and eighty miles. Our ship proves to be a good sea boat, and lays to in a gale beautifully. We have a good strong crew, but they are mostly foreigners. Sexton has had a good many of them under his care, but they are all well now. He has been very attentive to them, and, besides healing their bodies, has tried to do their souls good. One of them has been led, through his instrumentality, to see his sinfulness, to seek for mercy, and has now a hope in Jesus. God grant it may be that good hope 'which is as an anchor to the soul!' And now I should like to know if you and the family are well. Your miniature looks very natural; and, when we see it, we think how kind you were when we were last in Salem and how much you assisted us."

"March 7, 1848.

"My own dear Father, Mother, and Sisters,— Blessed be God, I can commence with the cheerful words, 'All is well.' We are now in what is called Pitts's Passage, leading through some of the many islands in the Indian Archipelago. Thus far the Lord has led us on in perfect safety: in the storm and in the calm he has been around us, and no evil has befallen us. We trust the same almighty arm has preserved you, and delivered you from every danger, and been your 'shield and buckler,' your ever-present guardian.

"Only think: I have crossed the equator twice, sailed over the Atlantic and Indian Oceans, and am now on the bosom of the vast Pacific. At midnight last night we passed the Pelew Islands, and to-day are sailing rapidly, being favored with a prosperous gale. I had expected to be sick again after getting out of the calms; but, thanks to my heavenly Father, I am not. I have felt a little unpleasantly with the increased motion, but that is all. Sexton has enjoyed remarkable health all the voyage. We are now beginning to desire most earnestly to be on land. I hardly know how we shall conduct ourselves on shore. I cannot think how land feels. And then we expect those precious home letters. God grant that they may be messengers of good tidings from the loved ones! If so, it seems to me that we shall be almost perfectly happy. May our hearts overflow with gratitude to

"'The glorious Giver, who doeth all things well.'"

"Hong Kong, March 26, 1848.

"My dearest Mother, — We anchored here last evening, and from our deck had a fine view of the place. This morning I awoke with different feelings from what I ever before experienced: my heart was never so grateful as when I knelt before the mercy seat and thanked God for his goodness and grace to us. Yes, we are safe; oceans have been crossed; and after one hundred and thirty-one days spent on the fathomless waters, we find ourselves safely moored on these heathen shores. O, do not let us doubt our heavenly Father's goodness, but trust him implicitly under all circumstances. The captain left us last night in the pilot boat and came off this morning, bringing to us precious letters; and we found truly that mother was a faithful correspondent. I feel almost as if I had seen you, these letters speak so loudly of home and home scenes. They are just the kind we want. There, too, I recognize father's handwriting and name. Tell him he must always write, if it is only five lines."

"Canton, April 9, 1848.

"My dear Mother, — I am alone in brother P.'s study, and thought I would sit down and talk a while with you. This is the holy Sabbath; but, when I look from the windows into the street below, I should not judge it holy time. Directly opposite is a bench on which meats are exposed for sale; and behind it stands a Chinaman, who is now drinking his favorite tea from his dear little cup. The next neighbor to this has an open store; and at the door Chinese cigars are displayed very attractively for the lovers of this article. They are little white things, resembling pipe stems. I have never taken one up to examine it. A constant procession of coolies is passing, bearing every imaginable kind of burden, hung on their never-failing bamboo. The Chinese invariably carry their fans with them; and it looks quite singular to an American to see them constantly used as screens. Women and girls of the lower classes are constantly passing; but as yet I have seen none of the higher order. Directly under my window is a grayhaired peddler, displaying his little stock of fruits, &c.

"At ten o'clock, A. M., we went down into the dining room with brother and sister P., and then took our seats around a long table, with Li-seen-Shang and two assistants. They all had the book of Matthew in Chinese; and the first teacher read aloud, and was followed by the others. Then, as all knelt together, one prayed. Next Li explained the parable of the ten virgins. Brother P. told us something of what he said. He appeared clearly to understand it. He said it resembled the marriage procession here, as they have very long ones, and carry lamps both in the day and night. He could well appreciate that parable. Sexton asked him several questions, to get at his ideas. He thought the servant who had 'one talent' was 'wicked and lazy,' and that, although he returned what the Lord gave him, he did not do his duty, because he should have improved it. After another prayer, the meeting closed.

"This was followed, at eleven o'clock, by a discourse from Li in the room used as a chapel. We were not there, but attended English services at Dr. Parker's. On the way we were met by throngs of people, and found it almost impossible to proceed, but fortunately found a gentleman friend who took us in charge. We learned that it was a great day here. Brother French, of the Presbyterian Board, preached from the words, 'What think ye of Christ?' It was a pleasant meeting, but very noisy without. We returned home safely, and brother P. told us there had been a gorgeous procession passing through the streets since we went out. All was then quiet. After dinner we sat and talked a while, and brother P. went below to get his little congregation together. He went to the door and beckoned some and urged others to come in. I could but think of that precious invitation, 'Ho, every one that thirsteth, come ye to the waters.' It was as if he had said,

'Come with us, and we will do you good.' We peeped out of the window at them, but could not go below, as they would look at us more than they would listen to the gospel. They got together a little company, and Li addressed them. I could hear his voice in earnest tones, but could not understand.

"I have just been at the window again; and several looked up, saw me, and laughed aloud, and some nodded; so I quietly turned back again, for a crowd would soon gather if I should stand there."

Her husband adds to this letter, —

"I went out yesterday to distribute books with brother Pearcy. We tried to enter the temple, but were repulsed. We distributed all the books we took out, and could have given away many more. The people are very willing to take books from us."

But the time was soon to come when these letters, so cheerfully written, were to end. The time was to come when the wife was to apply the truth of her own declaration to her husband previous to their union — "Thy people shall be my people, and thy God my God; where thou diest will I die, and there will I be buried." The same watery sepulchre was to enclose them both, and in each other's arms they were to go up to God. " Lovely in their lives, and not to be divided in death."

The sad manner of their deaths will be given in letters written to the afflicted parents by those who sympathized most deeply in the sad bereavement. These letters will explain themselves, and give a clearer view of the sad scenes which transpired, and a more vivid picture of what the feelings of the surviving missionaries must have been, than any language of ours. If the loss of Mr. and Mrs. James was felt any where, it must have been on the soil of China, and by those who were looking for the arrival and assistance of a physician and his companion with so much pleasure.

"Shanghai, July 13, 1848.

"My dear Brother, — The secretary of our mission here being so hurried to get every thing ready for sending by the present opportunity, it falls to my lot to communicate to you a copy of the following resolutions from our mission records. In sending them to you, I wish I could accompany them with one single word which might afford you and yours consolation under a bereavement so trying. But the truth is, the event has so stricken my own heart that I am little fitted to attempt to comfort others. It is to us, individually and as a mission, a dark providence; and we find ourselves even now, although months have elapsed, trying to realize that it is not so. We find, sometimes, relief even in our own delusions. And yet the tremendous reality of the thing is, alas! *irretrievably* settled. God grant us all the right kind of faith and true Christian submission in view of circumstances *so* overwhelming! But, my brother, God has indeed honored you, by enabling you, in the spirit of Abraham, to offer up your precious daughter for the spiritual, eternal welfare of China's perishing millions. You are one of *three* Baptist fathers whose beloved daughters have ended their honorable earthly career in China during 1848; and when the earth and the sea shall give up their sacred trusts, Mrs. Jarsom, of Ningpo, Mrs. Johnson, of Hong Kong, and *Mrs. James*, of Shanghai, will stand clothed in immortality around the great white throne. Yes, and three other female Baptist missionaries, — Mrs. Dean, *Mrs. Shuck*, and Mrs. Devan, — whose lovely forms now moulder on these distant heathen shores, shall rise with them and be forever with the Lord. I believe the lamented loss of dear Dr. and Mrs. James will call an attention to China and awaken an interest in the great work here which our kind and heavenly Father will overrule for the good of this people and the glory of his own name, so that, although dead, they will speak forth an influence in behalf of this vast empire, to whose welfare their lives were so early sacrificed. Yesterday we had the sincere though melancholy satisfaction of receiving an excellent daguerreotype of our beloved brother and sister, which is most gratifying to us all. Young-seen-sang was looking at them this morning, and returning the case to me, said, 'Roo chay, roo chay'—'Distressing, distressing.'

"At a meeting of the Shanghai Baptist Mission the following resolutions were passed:—

"'Whereas it has pleased our heavenly Father to deprive us of our beloved brother and sister, Dr. and Mrs. James, who were drowned by the sudden sinking of the schooner Paradox, at Hong Kong, April 15, 1848, on the eve of their embarkation for Shanghai to join us as colleagues in this mission, therefore

"'*Resolved*, that, while we endeavor to bow with meek submission to the all-wise doings of the great Lord of the harvest, the God of missions, we feel ourselves, as a mission and as individuals, deeply afflicted by this trying providence, which has with such awful suddenness torn from us those dear to us individually, and whom we regarded as so well qualified for the great and important work among the Gentiles in which they had come so far hence to engage.

"'*Resolved*, that we most truly sympathize with the bereaved parents and relatives of our dear deceased brother and sister, and also with the Board at Richmond, in view of the dark and mysterious providence which has overwhelmed us all in affliction and grief.

"'*Resolved*, that we send copies of these resolutions to the parents of our beloved but departed colleague in Philadelphia and Salem, and to the Board in Richmond, and that we have them inserted in the records of our mission, although we are assured that they inadequately express the warm sympathy and deep feelings of our hearts in reference to this solemn, unexpected, and afflictive bereavement.'

"In sending these resolutions to you, allow me to say that Mrs. Shuck and myself personally beg to assure you and your dear family of our sincerest sympathy and friendliness. May I trouble you for an acknowledgment of the receipt of this communication?

With every kind wish, believe me,
Faithfully and affectionately,
J. Lewis Shuck, *Chairman*."

"Hong Kong, April 22, 1848.

"My bereaved Sister,—It is with feelings of the deepest sympathy that I now address you on a subject which will rend your heart. Alas! alas! your beloved children, our dear brother and sister James, are *no more;* they have found a watery grave. Their bodies now lie in the bosom of the mighty deep, where they will remain until the resurrection morn, I fear. They wrote you by the last overland mail, informing you of their safe arrival at Hong

Kong on the 25th of March. On the 30th, in company with brother Dean, they left Hong Kong in the Valparaiso, and came up to Canton to make us a visit, as there was no prospect of their having an opportunity to go up the coast in two weeks or more. They reached Canton April 1, and we joyfully welcomed them to their field of labor. Brother Dean remained with us a week; they staid nearly two weeks, during which time we visited all the missionaries of the place in company with them; also most of the curiosities of the city. They were very pleasant and cheerful, and expressed themselves as being much pleased with their visit. We, on our part, were very much gratified to have them with us, and became quite attached to them during their visit.

" On the 13th instant, at nine o'clock P. M., they took an affectionate leave of us, and embarked on board the schooner Paradox, for Hong Kong, in accordance with previous arrangements which had been made by Dr. James in connection with two or three merchants who were going to Hong Kong and had chartered the schooner. We all congratulated ourselves on their having so safe and pleasant a passage in view; for the schooner was thought to be very safe, and had been much patronized heretofore. On the 15th, about ten o'clock A. M., just as they had come in sight of Hong Kong, (ten miles distant,) a sudden squall came up, and the schooner was immediately thrown on her side, filled with water, and sunk to the bottom, only a few feet of the masts being out of the water. Dr. and Mrs. James were in their cabin, and, I imagine, scarce had time to think ere they were enclosed in the water. The other passengers (four in number, besides several Chinese) were on deck: three were saved by clinging to the top of the mast until a boat which witnessed the occurrence came by and took them in. The other passenger, a youth from Philadelphia, named Ash, was drowned. Three Chinamen and a Chinese woman were also drowned. We received the sad intelligence at Canton on the following day between three and four o'clock P. M.; whereupon Mr. Pearcy and I soon set off in a fast boat, accompanied by Mr. Sword, uncle of Mr. Ash. When we arrived at Whampoa we took the little steamer Firefly, and arrived at Hong Kong at ten o'clock A. M. on the 17th instant. As we passed the place where the schooner was sunk, only a few feet of the mast were to be seen. Several boats were there; but nothing had been found but the body of the Chinese female. Brother and sister James are supposed to be still in the cabin. Strenuous efforts have been made for successive days to raise the schooner, but to no purpose. Chinese divers have been sent for, to procure the bodies if possible. It is thought to be rather a hopeless case, however.

"Truly it is a grievous disclosure of the divine will. We feel it keenly, and do most heartily sympathize with the relations and friends of the deceased. All the missionaries and friends here seem much concerned about it. Many prayers have been offered up on behalf of their relations, that our heavenly Father would afford them grace sufficient to bear up under the heavy stroke. I would fain offer you some consolation, but scarce know what to say. I can only point you to that book which alone is able to afford you consolation under such afflictive dispensations; and I feel assured you are no *stranger* to its comforts and promises.

"Let us not sorrow for them as for those that have no hope. They had it in their hearts to labor for the heathen; but God has otherwise directed. It is doubtless *all for the best*, though we cannot see *how*; perhaps we may hereafter. We thought them well qualified for the station assigned them, and hoped much good might be accomplished by them. We are all the Lord's; and surely he has a right to take whom he will, even those who seem to us to be best fitted to advance his cause on earth. May he sanctify the dispensation to you all! My dear husband unites in kind regards to all.

Your sister in Christ,
FRANCES M. PEARCY."

The following letter from James B. Taylor indicates the action of the Southern Board in relation to this most afflictive event:

"RICHMOND, July 29, 1848.

"MY DEAR BROTHER: Though personally unknown to you, I cannot refrain from giving vent to my feelings in relation to the very afflictive event which has torn so many hearts and called forth tears of bitter grief from so many eyes. When I heard of the sudden death of your beloved child and her companion I was from home, and the effect upon my mind was such that it was with extreme difficulty I could prosecute the duties before me. We had but a few days before heard of their safe arrival; the lines traced by the hand of your dear Annie had been read and re-read with lively interest. My own hopes with respect to her extensive usefulness had been excited, and I was looking forward to the period when, located in their chosen field of labor, they would both exercise a blessed influence in behalf of the wretched heathen. But these hopes have been disappointed. God has seen fit to cross our expectations. While we feel, and feel deeply, this heavy stroke, it is not right to repine. Their heavenly Father has taken them away. He loves *them* and the mission cause with a depth of affection of which our hearts are incapable. He sees it to be best — *best for them*, and best for the cause. Although we know not the precise design of this dispensation, yet *he* sees the end from the beginning, and, ordering all things after the counsel of his own will, has determined to remove them. They, in their heavenly home, doubtless perceive it (as we cannot) to be a wise and gracious dispensation. And O, how happy are they now, as they look upon the scenes of earth and contemplate the sovereignty of their adorable Redeemer, making all things to work together for good to his people and his cause!

"While I beg to present to your afflicted companion and yourself these considerations, considerations which have sustained my own heart, you will both accept my sincere condolence and sympathy in this the hour of your trial. The Lord, I trust, will comfort your hearts and sanctify the bereavement to your spiritual good.

"Since the above was written, at a full meeting of the Board the following resolutions were unanimously adopted:

" ' Whereas, the afflictive intelligence has reached the Board that Dr. J. Sexton James, and his lady, Mrs. Annie James, missionaries under their patronage, were suddenly cut off by death as they were proceeding from Canton to Hong Kong, therefore

" ' 1. *Resolved*, that the Board regard this dispensation of Providence as one of those mysterious events concerning which they are to find consolation only in the doctrine that the Lord reigneth, and, while clouds and darkness are round about him, righteousness and judgment are the habitation of his throne.

"'2. *Resolved,* that this event is well adapted to produce in the Board and among the churches an increased measure of the spirit of humiliation and prayer, thus preparing them to profit by the painful discipline to which the God of missions is subjecting them.

"'3. *Resolved,* that the Board cherish for the memory of their departed brother and sister the sincerest regard, and hereby tender to the bereaved parents and other relatives and friends their deep sympathy in this hour of painful affliction.

"'4. *Resolved,* that a copy of the above preamble and resolutions be forwarded to the parents of our brother and sister, and also be published in the Missionary Journal.'

"I shall be happy to receive a letter from you with any extracts from communications written by your *now glorified* Annie, which might be profitably inserted in our Missionary Journal."

In this sad manner, and with these testimonials of her goodness, departed one of the heroines of the Church to her long home, leaving behind her many friends who were sad and sorrowful at her decease. The following minute and solemn description of the melancholy event is found in a letter dated

"VICTORIA, April 22.

"Just as they came in sight of Hong Kong, on Saturday morning, the 15th instant, about ten o'clock, a gust of wind struck the schooner suddenly and with much force; and she instantly capsized, filled, and went down to the bottom with our dear brother James and his wife in the cabin. I can only say, 'It is the Lord: let him do what seemeth him good.' 'The Lord hath given and the Lord hath taken away: blessed be the name of the Lord.' Mr. Johnson and myself, with Mr. Pearcy, went to the spot to aid in recovering the bodies from the wreck. They have not yet been found; but there is some prospect of recovering them. The masts broke; and the divers say that they cannot go down in so deep water. We must send to Kechal for other divers.

"Mr. and Mrs. James were in the cabin at the time the schooner upset, the former having left the deck but a few minutes previous, where he had been conversing with Mr. Meigs. Captain Hedges, of the whale ship, who was a passenger, attributes the accident to want of skill on the part of the person having charge of the boat. At the time the squall struck her, her yards were braced so sharp, and the sails hauled so flat aft, the vessel refused to come up to the wind, but went over immediately upon her side. In a few minutes her stern commenced sinking, by the quantity of water taken in at the cabin companion way; and she went down stern foremost, leaving only the tops of her masts above the water. Nothing was seen of those who were in the cabin. All were saved who were on deck except Mr. Ash. The Canton larcha picked up the survivors, who were almost exhausted. Captain Hedges, who was clinging to the mast, says he could not have held on five minutes longer. He thinks the death of those in the cabin must have been instantaneous, by suffocation; for the cabin was so small as to be filled with one rush of water down the companion way. All the crew swam out. No noise was heard below except the air making its escape as the water filled the cabin. Four Chinese passengers were also drowned."

Here we have for our contemplation another instance of God's mysterious dealing with his people. Led on by his hand, this amiable young Christian left the home of her youth and went far away to labor for Christ; but, instead of this, her valuable life was taken from her, and her spirit ascended to God who gave it. When just about to become a useful laborer, the winds and waves conspired, and her hour came. In the arms of her husband she went up on high, and now stands among the ransomed; and in this little volume are recorded the mementoes of her worth and virtue.

CHAPTER XI.

EMILY C. JUDSON,

OF BURMAH.

WHEN the earlier editions of this work went to press, the heroine of this sketch was yet alive. Her record was not yet filled, her work was not yet done, and the measure of her usefulness was incomplete. Nor had her noble companion, whose name is identified with the great cause of Christian missions, found rest from his toils. Since then the name of Adoniram Judson has been transferred from the roll of the living to the long catalogue of the dead. The sea weed is his shroud, and the wild winds howl his requiem wildly and grandly. His gifted companion — she who left her early home, turned from the cottage of her mother, abandoned the walks and allurements of literature, and forsook her native land to cheer the last days of the mission soldier of the cross — has also been laid to rest. Her silent harp gives no utterance; her pen lies useless now; her body has been given to the dust; but her memory is fragrant, and, though dead, she lives in an accumulating influence, and in an imperishable memory. She was first known to the public as the teacher of a female seminary at Utica, New York, where she was much beloved by all who knew her. As a teacher she took a fair, respectable, but perhaps not an elevated position. She assumed the duties and responsibilities of the office, without experience, and young in years, and maintained her reputation as a faithful friend, a diligent instructer, and a gifted woman. While employed as teacher, she commenced the use of her pen, and, besides several newspaper and magazine articles, gave to the public a few religious books, which were published in the city of Philadelphia. And thus is introduced to us Miss Emily E. Chubbuck.

Miss Chubbuck was born in the pleasant town of Morrisville, in the central part of the State of New York. This is the Alderbrook of which mention is made so frequently in her writings, and for which she cherished such an ardent attachment. Here her attention was turned to the subject of religion; here she embraced the Savior; here she was consecrated to God in baptism, and by that holy rite signified her confession of Christ; and here united herself with a branch of the Christian church, to which she adhered until called up to unite with the church triumphant in heaven.

From Morrisville she removed to Utica, for the purpose of teaching, and there commenced, as before remarked, that brilliant literary career which has made her name familiar to all who love a pleasant tale and a good-natured story, told with exquisite grace and vivacity. Under a graceful *nom de plume* she gave to the public many a touching tale, written late at night, after the exhausting labors of the day were done, and the city was shrouded in darkness; and years before her real name was known to her readers, her *nom de plume* was familiar to young and old.

In 1844 she commenced writing for the New Mirror, then conducted in New York by N. P. Willis, who gladly availed himself of the labors of this gifted contributor. The articles published under the signature of "Fanny Forrester" were copied far and wide, and the author at once assumed a high rank among the magazine writers of the day. These articles have been freely condemned, and unjustly ranked with that class of books styled "novels," and which contain so much that is vitiating to the public taste and degrading to the public heart. Those who condemn all fictitious works, and who can see but little good in any thing besides dry details and stern facts, were ready to condemn the authoress, who, to support an aged mother, and to do good, entered a walk in literature which has since been trodden by many others, who have reaped therein a rich pecuniary harvest. By these persons the choice made by Dr. Judson in the selection of a companion was deemed injudicious. But these feelings were cherished, these thoughts expressed, generally, by those who had not read the writings of Fanny Forrester, or who had no taste for the beautiful sympathy of these life-like tales. Hundreds of Christians have perused "Alderbrook," and arisen from the task with more correct views of human life, and a stronger determination to labor for God and humanity.

The motive which prompted her to pen these articles was a high and holy one. By the providence of God, a mother had been left somewhat dependent upon her care, and as she wrote, and heard the voice of deserved commendation, that voice was mingled with the sweet tones of Jesus — "Behold thy mother." Conscience approved, and the idea of repaying the care and anxiety of parental love was more grateful to the young maiden than the plaudits of the crowd. And in all that she wrote, it is believed that no error is to be found, no bitter drops to poison the mind, but under the thin garb of fiction much of that pure morality which the Bible alone imparts, and which religion so highly commends.

In 1848, the Memoir of Sarah B. Judson was issued from the press. Differing entirely from the beautiful Memoir of the first Mrs. Judson, prepared by Prof. Knowles, and perhaps not justly termed a *memoir*, yet as a *sketch* of life and character, it is a book of much merit. It is written in a style calculated to draw the attention and win the affections of the reader, and will doubtless be read by hundreds who would never have opened the leaves of the volume, had it been prepared in the usual style of religious biographies. We are aware that it can have no place among standard biographical works, and that the view of Mrs. Judson, who was a plain, matter-of-fact woman, is taken too generally from the standpoint of the poetess. Yet the volume, though of little worth as a reliable narrative of facts, is of much importance as a series of life pictures, calculated to inspire the heart and move the soul to womanly deeds.

The true portrait of Fanny Forrester will be given by herself in her own writings; and the best method of exhibiting the features of her mind, and the characteristics of her literary taste, is to present the delicate, charming sentences she wrote. How beautifully from "Underhill Cottage" does she describe her own "Alderbrook!" "I am not sure," she says, "that there are any angels here; but the flowers sometimes have a look to them that makes me afraid to break their stems; and there are moments when it would require infinite daring to toss a pebble into the brook; for who can tell but it might hush one of those voices that sing to me in the holy solitude? The trees, too, have a strange lovingness, leaning over the brook protectingly, and shadowing the little violets, as many a high spirit stoops to watch over a poor human blossom. O, there are beating pulses in the trees, and I love them, because I know there is a Great Heart somewhere that keeps them all in motion. Perhaps —— But you shall not be told all the things that have been whispered in my ear by those fresh-lipped leaves, when not a mortal foot was nearer than the far-off road; though feet enow were tripping it over the grass blades, and a listener sat perched on every spray. Page on page of spirit lore have I gathered there; but I have closed the book now, and 'clasped it with a clasp.' That is my wealth, and I am a miser.

"Come to Alderbrook, I say, *in the spring time*, for the crackle of the wood fire, by which I am writing, might be a music which would scarce please you; and, sooth to say, our winter cheer offers little that is inviting to a pleasure-seeker. It is well to take to the turf when you reach the toll-gate at the foot of the hill: for the road has a beautiful green margin to it, grateful to feet sick of the dust of a day's ride. It is not a difficult walk to the top, as I well know; having climbed it a score of times every year, since first I chased a playful little racer of a squirrel along the crooked fence, fully persuaded that there *was* some sudden way of taming it, notwithstanding its evident scorn of the peeled nut, which I held coaxingly between my thumb and forefinger. High hills, skirted by forests, are rising on the right; and on the left is a slope, terminating in a deep gorge, through which the little brook tinkles, as though myriads of fairy revellers tripped it there, to the music of their own silver bells. Perched on the top of the hill is a tall, weather-painted house, of a contracted make, though, like some people, whose mental dimensions have been narrowed, with a very smart, uppish air about it; and fronting it, away down in a deep, wild ravine, is an old, moss-grown saw-mill. It has been forsaken this many a long year; the wheel is broken, and the boards are rotting away; but yet it is verily believed by many, that the old saw still uses its rusty teeth o' nights, and that strange, unholy guests keep wassail there, at the expense of a poor mortal long since mouldering in his shroud. Alas for thee, old Jake Gawesley! It was a fearful thing to raise such a pile of worldly possessions between thyself and humanity! How gladly wouldst thou, in that last hour, have bought, with the whole of them, a single love-softened hand to soothe, with such a touch as love only knows, thy throbbing temple! O, it is a horrible thing to turn from the world, and bear not away the pure passport of a mourner's tear. Thy grave has never been watered by the dews distilled from a human heart, like the flower-planted ones around it; the small gray stone at its head is broken, and no one cares to replace it; and the thistle nods to the wind above thee. It is said that this sawmill was erected on an orphan's rights; and men are as fond of the doctrine of retribution as though they never sinned. Hence the superstition.

"You will see, from this point, the little village of Alderbrook, so near that you may count every house in it. There are two pretty churches — one on the top of the rise called 'The Hill,' the other nestled down in a very sweet spot on 'The Flat.' Then we have, besides, the seminary, made memorable by poor Jem Fletcher; a district school house, painted red; and a milliner's shop, painted yellow; three stores, two taverns, (one with a sign-post, once tantalizing to my young eyes, so candy-like did it look in its coat of white, with a wisp of crimson about it,) a printing office, in which the 'Alderbrook Sun' rises of a Wednesday morning; a temple of Vulcan, and two or three other establishments, sacred to the labors of our native artisans."

In all her writings there is a gladness, an ease, a freedom, *an inexpressible something*, which makes even the heart of an old man large within him, and brings gladness even to the torn bosom of sorrow and want. All her articles are characterized by womanly pity for the fallen and sympathy with the erring; and there is not one in which the true spirit of philanthropy and kindness does not appear. There is an artlessness, a sympathy, which makes us feel that we are reading lessons from the pen of one who has the honesty of a little child. We may readily believe her when she says, speaking of her young playmate, Charley Hill, " Pity that we cannot always be children. It is a very uncomfortable thing to be dignified and proper; and I would advise every child to put a stone on his head to keep him from growing, if by so doing he may keep the stone from falling on his heart."

In the poetic contributions of our heroine to literature, there is the same sweetness and delicacy of expression, as will be seen from the following article, one of her earlier poems, entitled " THE TWO FLOWERS."

> A flower peeped out from the fields of green,
>   Which had long about it lain;
> A dainty thing in purple sheen,
>   Without a blight or stain.
> A brighter bud ne'er burst, I ween,
>   In bower, on hill, or plain.
>
> And the breeze came out and kissed its lip,
>   And the sun looked in its eye;
> And the golden bee, its sweets to sip,
>   Kept all day buzzing by;
> There chose the grasshopper to skip,
>   There glanced the butterfly.

A human soul from that young flower
  Seemed glorying in the light;
And when came on the mellow hour,
  The blossom still was bright;
And then there crept around the bower
  A dark and solemn night.

Gay dawn her portals open flung,
  But the floweret looked not up;
There on its light-poised stem it hung,
  A tear within its cup;
Close to its heart the woe-drop clung,
  And the floweret looked not up.

The winning breezes whispered round,
  Warm sun-rays came a-wooing,
And bright-winged, bliss-born things were found
  Beside its petals suing;
But the flower bent lower to the ground,
  Those petals on it strewing.

And when I saw the blossom dead
  Upon the dewy sod,
I thought of one whose bright young head
  Is pillowed by the clod;
Who staid one sorrowing tear to shed,
  Then bore it to her God.

Miss Chubbuck employed her pen in this pleasing and profitable manner, until called in the providence of God to fill another and a nobler sphere of Christian usefulness, as the companion of one who had won imperishable laurels on the field of Christian heroism. In 1846, Dr. Judson returned from India to America, and was now introduced to the sweet, amiable, gentle Fanny Forrester, as a suitable person to write the memoir of Mrs. Sarah B. Judson, his late beloved companion. To this work reference has been had, and Miss Chubbuck undertook the task; and being necessarily in the company of each other much of the time, a mutual affection ripened between them; and when the hour came for Judson to return to the land of his labors and sorrows, the favored child of literature consented to accompany him as his companion and helper.

They were married at Hamilton, N. Y., by Rev. Dr. Kendrick, on the 2d day of June, 1846. Just before leaving America, she penned the following farewell address to loved friends and loved scenes: —

"In dissevering the various ties which bind me to the land of my birth, I find one of peculiar strength and interest. It is not easy to say farewell, when father and mother, brother and sister, and those scarce less dear, are left behind us at the word; it is not easy to break away from the sweet, simple attractions of social life, or the increasing fascinations of a world but too bright and beautiful; but there are other ties to break, other sorrowful farewells to be spoken. The parents and friends, brothers and sisters, whom Christ has given us, and who for his sake have loved us, occupy no remote corner of our hearts. Such friends of mine are, I trust, scattered over various parts of the country — those whose prayers are at this very moment strengthening both hand and heart. O, I know ye have prayed for me, ye whose prayers 'avail much;' for, casting away my broken reed, and trusting in God only, I have been made strong.

"We do not always feel the deepest love for those with whom we are visibly connected; so, though the beloved church in the village of Hamilton has never been my home, the strongest tie binding me to it, is not that the names of those to whom God first gave me are enrolled among its members. I have often worshipped there; there a resolution, a consecration of self, — which cost, the Omniscient only knows how great an effort, — received ready encouragement and sympathy; there prayers were offered, tears were shed, and blessings spoken, which I shall bear upon my heart, a precious burden; and thither I shall turn for future prayers, future encouragement, and future sympathy. O, my eyes grow dim when I think of the loved ones, friends of Jesus, in my own dear home — the beautiful village of Hamilton.

"There is another church with whom I have a more intimate connection — the one whose commendation I bear to a strange people, in a strange land, but worshipping no strange God.

"There are to me no dearer ones on earth than a little circle at Utica, with whom I have hoped and feared, rejoiced, and wept, and prayed. God grant that I may join that same circle above! that the tremulous voice which thousands of times has borne a confession of our sins and follies up to our Intercessor, I may hear again in songs of praise; that when the thin, gray hairs are brightened, and the heavy foot made swift and light, I may return heavenly love for the counsels to which I have so often listened. I do not *ask* to be remembered there, for I know that parting in person cannot mar the union of the spirit; and when my hand is strong, and my heart light, when Christ confers upon me any peculiar blessing, I shall think that Deacon Sheldon, and those who love him and me, are praying for me.

" There is another little church worshipping God quietly away in an obscure village: and with that church, before all others, I claim my home. All the associations of childhood cluster there; and there still sparkle the bright waters where the revered Chinese missionary, now on his way back to the scence of his labors, administered the initiatory rite of the church, when she consented to receive the trembling, doubting child into her bosom. O, the church at Morrisville, the sober, prayerful ones who were my first Christian guides, must let my heart have a home among them still. There are my Christian fathers and mothers, my teachers in the Sabbath school, and those whom I have taught;

the dearest, sweetest associations of life cluster around the little missionary society, the evening Bible class, the prayer circle in which I first mingled; and the little plans for doing good in which I was allowed to participate, when I first loved my Savior, are as fresh in memory as though formed yesterday.

"Dear friends of Jesus at Morrisville, ye whose prayers first drew me to the protection of your church, — whose prayers sustained me through the many years that I remained with you, — whose prayers, I trust, have followed me during the little time that we have been separated, — will you pray for me still? When dangers and difficulties are about me, will you plead earnestly, 'God help her!' Will you pray for me, now that we are to see each other's faces no more in this world? Ah, I know you will; so let me ask the same for those among whom I go to labor; those who know not Christ and his salvation, and yet 'are without excuse.' Pray for them, and for me, that I may do them good. EMILY JUDSON."

A farewell service was held at Baldwin Place Church, of the most solemn and interesting character, and seven devoted servants of God covenanted to go out to a world in darkness. The farewell words of Dr. Judson, after his address had been read by Rev. Mr. Hague, were, —

"I wish, however, with my own voice, to praise God for the proofs which he has given of his interest in missions; and to thank you from the bottom of my heart for the kindness which I have received from you. I regret that circumstances beyond my control have prevented my being much in this city, to make more intimate acquaintance with those whom a slight acquaintance has taught me so much to love. I am soon to depart; and, as is in the highest degree probable, never to return. I shall no more look upon this beautiful city — no more visit your temples, or see your faces. I have one favor to ask of you. Pray for me, and for my associates in the missionary work; and though we meet no more on earth, may we at last meet where the loved and the parted here below meet never to part again."

Rev. H. A. Graves thus describes the scene which occurred upon the wharf when the vessel which was to bear away the precious freight loosened herself from the shore and swung out into the harbor: —

"We have now, at the writing of this, — Saturday afternoon, at one o'clock, — just returned from being witnesses of a scene that can never fade from the vision. At the foot of Central Wharf, a large company, despite the oppressive heat of the weather, had collected, many of whom had stood on the ground for hours, that they might exchange the parting salutation, and catch the parting look of the loved and the venerated, going far hence to the heathen, 'to them that sit in darkness, in the region and shadow of death.' An appropriate and fervent prayer was offered by Rev. A. D. Gillette, of Philadelphia, and a beautiful hymn, written for the occasion, by Mrs. Edmond, was then sung. The voice of prayer, the sounds of music, hallowed by such a scene, who can ever forget?

"On a small, raised platform, as the noble vessel, the 'Faneuil Hall,' was loosed from her moorings, stood the little group of missionaries, with him, their pioneer and chief, and her who, in fidelity to Christ, accompanies him, conspicuous to the view. Rev. Adoniram Judson, D. D., and Mrs. Emily Judson, Rev. John S. Beecher and wife, Rev. Norman Harris and wife, and Miss Lydia Lillybridge, were the company.

> 'Bear them on, thou restless ocean,
> Let the winds their canvas swell.'

"Before a sweet and favoring breeze, the ship bore them away as if proud of her treasure, and the cloud of waving signals from the sea and the shore soon disappeared from the sight. The face of each missionary, so far as we could discern, wore a cheerful aspect, as if the smile and the love of Jesus, for whose sake they had given themselves up to this service, were, during these very moments, richly enjoyed. None appeared more so than she to whom her own sweet lines find now so fit an application : —

> ' I shrink not from the shadows sorrow flings
>   Across my pathway ; nor from cares that rise
> In every footprint ; for each shadow brings
>   Sunshine and rainbow as it glooms and flies.
>
> ' But heaven is dearer. There I have my treasure ;
>   There angels fold in love their sunny wings ;
> There sainted lips chant in celestial measure,
>   And spirit-fingers stray o'er heaven-wrought strings.
>
> ' Then let me die. My spirit longs for heaven,
>   In its pure bosom evermore to rest ;
> But if to labor longer here be given,
>   " Father, thy will be done ! " and I am blest.' "

Mrs. Judson arrived in safety, and after passing through various trials, which she bore with cheerful resignation, was somewhat comfortably located in her new home. Near the close of 1847, she gave birth to a daughter, which suggested the following beautiful poem, which has been published extensively in this country : —

MY BIRD.

> Ere last year's moon had left the sky,
>   A birdling sought my Indian nest,
> And folded, O, so lovingly !
>   Her tiny wings upon my breast.

From morn till evening's purple tinge,
  In winsome helplessness she lies;
Two rose leaves with a silken fringe,
  Shut softly on her starry eyes.

There's not in Ind a lovelier bird;
  Broad earth owns not a happier nest;
O God, thou hast a fountain stirred,
  Whose waters never more shall rest!

This beautiful, mysterious thing,
  This seeming visitant from Heaven,
This bird with the immortal wing,
  To me — to me thy hand has given.

The pulse first caught its tiny stroke,
  The blood its crimson hue, from mine: —
This life, which I have dared invoke,
  Henceforth is parallel with thine.

A silent awe is in my room —
  I tremble with delicious fear;
The future, with its light and gloom,
  Time and eternity are here.

Doubts, hopes, in eager tumult rise;
  Hear, O my God, one earnest prayer: —
Room for my bird in Paradise,
  And give her angel plumage there!

For a while the heroic missionary woman cheered the home of her husband, or labored by his side in the wilds of heathenism, until, by failing health, Dr. Judson was admonished of his approaching end. A sea voyage was recommended; and on board the Aristide Marie, he embarked in April, 1850, in company with a male friend, with the vain hope of securing that health which eluded him on the land. But death met him on the deep, and after days of anguish, the spirit of the good man fled away to God. There was a funeral at sea, and on the land a weeping widow. The sable-clad mother gathered her children, and came back to the friends of her youth, where she was received with that warm sympathy which her case demanded.

But she did not long survive her noble husband. She settled up his affairs, saw his Memoirs published, his children cared for, *and then died.* Literature opened its arms to welcome her again to the rewards of genius and the wreaths of fame; religion pointed her to new fields of labor in the land of her fathers; affection kindled new fires on the old hearth-stone: but her work was done, and God called her up to meet her sainted husband in glory. O, what a meeting that must have been, when from Amherst, St. Helena, America, and from the deep ocean, four redeemed ones met before the throne of God, to be parted no more. And here our record closes, with the close of a beautiful life, sheened, doubtless, by her devotion to the cause of the suffering Savior, and the work to which, with the noble spirit of a martyr, she devoted herself. She did not tread the dungeon path, as did the pious woman, who, on board the Caravan, set sail with the pioneer from the harbor of Salem. She went not to Oung-pen-la with blistered feet: she hung not over a beloved form, chained and sick at Maloun: she was not even permitted to close the eyes of him she loved, and yet she was no less a heroine of faith, and worthy of an enduring record.

We now close the volume. Here are grouped the names of several estimable women, of different sects, and of various degrees of culture, all of whom are now at rest. Well would it be if all the daughters of the cross would emulate the bright example left for them by their missionary sisters of charity, and, though not called out to other lands to die amid strangers, yet here at home develop those high virtues and those noble traits for which this cluster of Christians have become so widely and justly distinguished.